MathFlare

Name: ______________________

Class: ___________

Teacher: ______________________

Introduction

As parents and educators, we recognize the pivotal role mathematics plays in shaping a child's academic journey and future success. Yet, the path to mathematical proficiency can often seem daunting, fraught with challenges and complexities. That's where the transformative power of MathFlare Workbooks shine through, illuminating the way forward with clarity, precision, and purpose.

Introducing MathFlare Workbooks – a beacon of guidance, a testament to excellence, and a catalyst for achievement. Crafted with meticulous care and expertise, MathFlare Workbooks stand as paragons of educational excellence, designed to nurture young minds, ignite a passion for learning, and develop a deep-rooted understanding of mathematical concepts.

Picture this: your child eagerly delves into the pages of Mathflare Workbook, greeted by a step-by-step guide illuminated with vivid examples that demystify complex mathematical concepts. With each turn of the page, they embark on a journey of discovery, encountering thoughtfully curated practice questions that reinforce learning and hone problem-solving skills. And when they unveil the answers to those very questions, a sense of accomplishment blossoms within them – a tangible reward for their hard work and dedication.

But MathFlare Workbooks are more than just tools for learning; they are pathways to comprehension, fostering a deep-seated understanding of mathematical concepts through a sequential, logical flow. From fundamental principles to advanced problem-solving strategies, every chapter builds upon the last, ensuring a robust foundation upon which future knowledge can be constructed.

As parents, we yearn for nothing more than to see our children thrive, to witness the spark of inspiration ignited within them as they conquer academic challenges with confidence and poise. MathFlare Workbooks serve as partners in this noble endeavor, offering not just practice questions, but the keys to unlocking a world of opportunity.

And for teachers, MathFlare Workbooks stand as invaluable allies in the quest to cultivate mathematical proficiency in the classroom. With answers readily available, instructors can focus on guiding and nurturing their students, confident in the knowledge that MathFlare Workbooks provide a solid framework upon which to build.

In the pages of MathFlare Workbooks, we find not just the promise of academic excellence, but the seeds of a brighter tomorrow. So let us embrace the power of mathematics, let us champion the journey of learning, and let us pave the way for a generation of young minds poised to shape the world. With MathFlare Workbooks as our guide, the possibilities are infinite, and the future, bright.

Table of Contents

MathFlare
MATH WORKBOOK
Grade 2
Step by Step Guide and Essential Practice with Answers
Addition Subtraction
Multiplication
Place Value and Expanded Notations
Geometry
MathFlare Publishing

MathFlare
MATH WORKBOOK
Grade 2-3
Step by Step Guide and Essential Practice with Answers
Addition Subtraction
Multiplication and Division
Place Value and Expanded Notations
Geometry
MathFlare Publishing

MathFlare
MATH WORKBOOK
Grade 3
Step by Step Guide and Essential Practice with Answers
Multiplication and Division
Decimals
Place Value and Expanded Notations
Fractions and Geometry
MathFlare Publishing

MathFlare
MATH WORKBOOK
Grade 1
Step by Step Guide and Essential Practice with Answers
Counting and Numbers
Addition and Subtraction
Place Value and Expanded Notations
Understanding Time
MathFlare Publishing

MathFlare
MATH WORKBOOK
Grade 1-2
Step by Step Guide and Essential Practice with Answers
Counting and Numbers
Addition and Subtraction
Place Value and Expanded Notations
Understanding Time
MathFlare Publishing

MathFlare
MATH WORKBOOK
Grade 3-4
Step by Step Guide and Essential Practice with Answers
Addition Subtraction
Multiplication Division
Place Value and Expanded Notations
Fractions and Geometry
MathFlare Publishing

MathFlare
MATH WORKBOOK
Grade 4
Step by Step Guide and Essential Practice with Answers
Addition Subtraction
Multiplication Division
Place Value and Expanded Notations
Fractions and Geometry
MathFlare Publishing

MathFlare
MATH WORKBOOK
Grade 4-5
Step by Step Guide and Essential Practice with Answers
Multiplication Division
Place Value and Expanded Notations
Fractions and Geometry
Unit Conversion
MathFlare Publishing

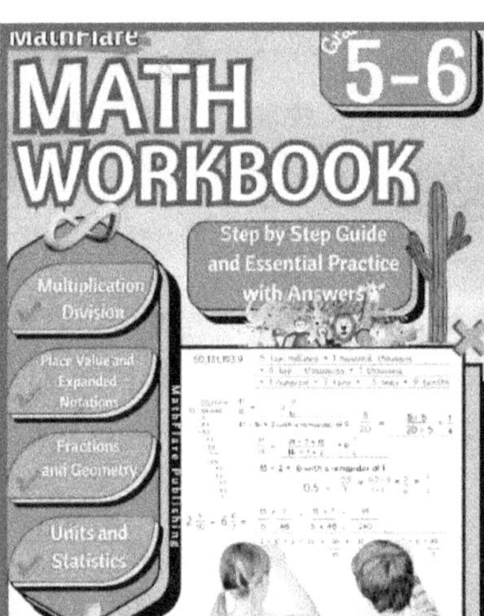

Decimals

Adding Decimals

Adding decimals is like adding whole numbers, but we must align the decimal points carefully. For instance, when adding 49.88 and 45.78:

Step 1: Align the decimal points.

$$49.88$$
$$+\ 45.78$$

Step 2: Start adding from the rightmost digit (the ones place) and move to the left.

Add 8 and 8: 8 + 8 = 16. Write down 6 in the ones place and carry over 1 to the tenths place.

$$49.88$$
$$+\ 45.78$$
$$6$$

Step 3: Add the tenths place.

Add 1 (carried over from the previous step), 8, and 7: 1 + 8 + 7 = 16. Write down 6 in the tenths place and carry over 1 to the hundredths place.

$$49.88$$
$$+\ 45.78$$
$$66$$

Step 4: Continue adding digits to the left until you reach the leftmost digit:

$$49.88$$
$$+\ 45.78$$
$$9566$$

<u>Step 5: Finally, write the sum with the decimal point directly below the decimal points in the original numbers.</u>

$$49.88 \\ +\ 45.78 \over 95.66$$

Let's solve a problem:

$$835.68 \\ +\ 825.29 \over 1,660.97$$

Subtracting Decimals

Subtracting decimals follows a process like adding decimals, except instead of adding the numbers, we subtract them.

For example:

$$697.05 \\ -\ 258.40 \over 438.65$$

Multiplying Decimals

Multiplying decimals is a lot like multiplying whole numbers, but we need to be careful about where we put the decimal point in the answer.

Step 1: Start by multiplying the numbers together, just like we do with whole numbers. Ignore the decimals for now.

Step 2: Count how many decimal places there are in the numbers we're multiplying. This will tell us how many decimal places our answer should have.

Step 3: Put the decimal point in the answer by starting from the right side of the number. Move the decimal point to the left as many places as there are in the total number of decimal places.

For example, let's multiply 4.5 by 2.5:

Step 1: Multiply the numbers as if they were whole numbers:

$$25 \times 45 = 1125.$$

Step 2: There is one decimal place in 2.5 and one in 4.5, making a total of two decimal places.

Step 3: Starting from the right side of the answer, count two places to the left and put the decimal point there.

So, the final answer is 11.25.

Remember to pay close attention to where the decimal point goes in the answer.

Let's solve a problem:

$$
\begin{array}{r}
85.39 \\
\times \quad 1.44 \\
\hline
+ \quad 34156 \\
+ \quad 34156 \\
+ \quad 8539 \\
\hline
= 122.9616
\end{array}
$$

Dividing Decimals

Dividing decimals is a lot like dividing whole numbers, but we need to be careful about placement of decimal point in the answer.

Steps to follow:

1. **Set up the division problem:** Write the dividend (the number being divided) and the divisor (the number you're dividing by) as you would in a long division problem.

$$1.7 \overline{)1.6}$$

2. **Move the decimal:** Move the decimal point to the right in the dividend and divisor by the same number of places.

$$17 \overline{)16}$$

3. **Perform the division:** Divide as you would with whole numbers.

$$
\begin{array}{r}
0\,0.9\,4 \\
17\overline{)16} \\
-\ 0 \\
\hline
1\,6 \\
-\ 0 \\
\hline
1\,6\,0 \\
-1\,5\,3 \\
\hline
7\,0 \\
-\ 6\,8 \\
\hline
2
\end{array}
$$

4. **Place the decimal point:** Place the decimal point in the quotient directly above its position in the dividend.

So, the quotient is 0.94.

Let's solve another problem:

$$
\begin{array}{r}
4.567 \\
12\overline{)\,54.8} \\
\end{array}
$$

```
        4.567
  12 ) 54.8
       - 0
        5 4
      - 4 8
        6 8
      - 6 0
        8 0
      - 7 2
        8 0
      - 7 2
          8
```

Using the Power of 10

Using the powers of 10, 100, and 1000 makes multiplying and dividing by these numbers very convenient. Let's illustrate with examples:

Multiplying by Powers of 10:

- To multiply a number by 10, simply move the decimal point one place to the right.

$$5 \times 10 = 50$$

- To multiply a number by 100, move the decimal point two places to the right.

$$5 \times 100 = 500$$

- To multiply a number by 1000, move the decimal point three places to the right.

$$5 \times 1000 = 5000.$$

Dividing by Powers of 10:

- To divide a number by 10, simply move the decimal point one place to the left.

$$50 \div 10 = 5$$

- To divide a number by 100, move the decimal point two places to the left.

$$500 \div 100 = 5$$

- To divide a number by 1000, move the decimal point three places to the left.

$$5000 \div 1000 = 5$$

Fractions

Fractions represent parts of a whole. They consist of a numerator (the number on top) and a denominator (the number on the bottom).

For example: we have an orange, and we divide it into 5 equal slices. Each slice represents $\frac{1}{5}$ of the orange. Now, if we take 3 of those slices, we have taken $\frac{3}{5}$ of the orange.

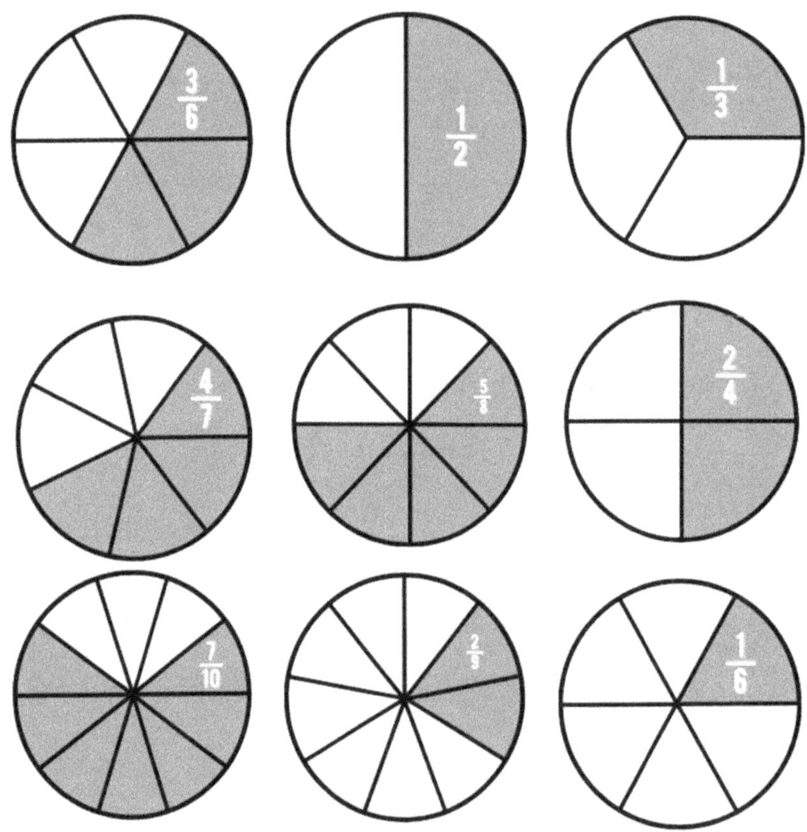

Equivalent Fractions

Equivalent fractions are fractions that represent the same value or part of a whole, even though they may look different.

To find equivalent fractions, you can:

- Multiply or divide both the numerator and denominator by the same nonzero number.
- Simplify fractions to their simplest form.

$\frac{1}{2}$ and $\frac{2}{4}$ are equivalent fractions because if you multiply the numerator and denominator of $\frac{1}{2}$ by 2, you get $\frac{2}{4}$. Similarly, if you divide both the numerator and denominator of $\frac{2}{4}$ by 2, you get $\frac{1}{2}$.

Let's solve a problem:

$$\frac{}{8} = \frac{15}{40}$$

To solve the missing numerator, we can cross multiply.

$$40x = 8 \times 15$$

$$40x = 120$$

$$x = \frac{120}{40} = x = 3$$

$$\frac{3}{8} = \frac{15}{40}$$

Convert Fractions and Decimals

To transform a fraction into a decimal, we divide the numerator by the denominator.

For instance, $\frac{1}{4}$ equals 0.25 because when we divide 1 by 4, we get 0.25.

In certain cases, the resulting decimal repeats infinitely, like $\frac{1}{3}$, which equals 0.3333...

In such instances, we round the decimal to a specific number of decimal places.

Let's solve a problem:

$$\frac{52}{100} = \underline{0.52}$$

Least Common Multiple (LCM)

The Lowest Common Multiple (LCM) of two or more numbers is the smallest multiple that is divisible by each of the numbers.

There are several methods to find the LCM; however, we will focus on only two:

Listing Multiples: List the multiples of each number until you find a common multiple. For example:

$$
\begin{array}{r}
8 \quad \underline{8,\ 16,\ 24,\ 32,\ 40,\ 48,\ 56} \\
7 \quad \underline{7,\ 14,\ 21,\ 28,\ 35,\ 42,\ 49,\ 56}
\end{array}
, \text{ LCM} = \underline{56}
$$

Division Method: Divide each number with the smallest prime number that divides at least one of the numbers evenly. The product of all the divisors and quotients is the LCM. For example:

$$
\begin{array}{c|cc}
2 & 7 & 8 \\
\hline
2 & 7 & 4 \\
\hline
2 & 7 & 2 \\
\hline
7 & 7 & 1 \\
\hline
  & 1 & 1
\end{array}
$$

$$\text{LCM} = 2 \times 2 \times 2 \times 7 = \underline{56}$$

Both methods have their advantages. For big numbers, using the division way is usually faster. But if we are working with smaller numbers or like seeing patterns, listing multiples might make more sense.

Fractions Multiplication

To multiply fractions, we simply multiply the numerators together to get the new numerator and multiply the denominators together to get the new denominator.

For example, let's multiply: $\frac{2}{4} \times \frac{1}{4}$

$$\text{Numerator: } 2 \times 1 = 2$$

$$\text{Denominator: } 4 \times 4 = 16$$

$$\text{Therefore, } \frac{2}{16}$$

$$\text{we can simplify the resulting fraction: } \frac{1}{8}$$

Let's solve a problem:

$$\frac{4}{5} \times \frac{4}{5} = \frac{4 \times 4}{5 \times 5} = \frac{16}{25}$$

Fractions Division

To divide fractions, we multiply by the reciprocal of the divisor.

For example, let's divide:

$$\frac{6}{8} \div \frac{4}{8}$$

$$\frac{6}{8} \times \frac{8}{4} = \frac{48}{32} = \frac{3}{2}$$

<u>Mixed Numbers: Mixed into Improper</u>

Mixed numbers and improper fractions are two different ways to represent the same value of a fraction.

1. **Mixed Number:** A mixed number is a combination of a whole number and a proper fraction. For example, $2\frac{1}{3}$ is a mixed number, where 2 is the whole number part and $\frac{1}{3}$ is the fraction part.

2. **Improper Fraction:** An improper fraction is a fraction where the numerator is greater than or equal to the denominator. For example, $\frac{7}{3}$ is an improper fraction because 6 is greater than 3.

To convert a mixed number to an improper fraction, you multiply the whole number by the denominator of the fraction, add the numerator, and then write the result over the original denominator. For example:

$$2\frac{1}{3} = \frac{2 \times 3 + 1}{3} = \frac{7}{3}$$

To convert an improper fraction to a mixed number, we divide the numerator by the denominator. The quotient becomes the whole number part, and the remainder becomes the numerator of the fraction. For example:

$$\frac{7}{3} = 2\frac{1}{3}$$

Let's solve some problems:

$$2 \frac{10}{20} = \begin{array}{l} 20 \times 2 = 40 \\ 40 + 10 = 50 \end{array} = \frac{50}{20} = \frac{5}{2}$$

$$\frac{41}{16} = 2 \frac{9}{16}$$

$$41 \div 16 = 2 \text{ with a remainder of } 9$$

Mixed Numbers: Addition and Subtraction

To add or subtract mixed numbers, we follow similar steps as when adding or subtracting regular fractions. For instance:

Addition:

- Add the whole numbers: Add the whole number parts of the mixed numbers together.
- Add the fractions: Add the fractions parts of the mixed numbers together.
- Simplify (if needed): If the fraction part of the sum is an improper fraction, simplify it by converting it to a mixed number.

Subtraction:

- Subtract the whole numbers: Subtract the whole number part of the second mixed number from the whole number part of the first mixed number.
- Subtract the fractions: Subtract the fraction part of the second mixed number from the fraction part of the first mixed number.
- Simplify (if needed): If the fraction part of the difference is a negative fraction, borrow from the whole number part or simplify it by converting it to a mixed number.

Let's solve some problems:

$$3\frac{4}{8} + 7\frac{1}{3} = \frac{4}{8} + \frac{1}{3} = \frac{4\times3 + 8\times1}{8\times3} = \frac{12 + 8}{24} = \frac{20}{24} = 10\frac{5}{6}$$

$$3 + 7 = 10$$

$$7\frac{4}{6} - 2\frac{3}{8} = \frac{4}{6} - \frac{3}{8} = \frac{4\times8 - 6\times3}{6\times8} = \frac{32 - 18}{48} = \frac{14}{48} = 5\frac{7}{24}$$

$$7 - 2 = 5$$

Mixed Numbers: Multiplication and Division

To multiply or divide mixed numbers, we follow these steps:

Multiplication:

- <u>Convert the mixed numbers to improper fractions</u>: Multiply the whole number by the denominator of the fraction, then add the numerator. Write the result over the original denominator.
- <u>Multiply the fractions</u>: Multiply the numerators together to get the new numerator and multiply the denominators together to get the new denominator.
- <u>Simplify (if needed)</u>: If the result is an improper fraction, simplify it by converting it back to a mixed number.

Division:

- <u>Convert the mixed numbers to improper fractions:</u>
- <u>Invert the divisor</u>: Flip the second fraction (the one you're dividing by) so that the division becomes multiplication.
- <u>Multiply the fractions</u>: Multiply the numerators together to get the new numerator and multiply the denominators together to get the new denominator.

- <u>Simplify (if needed)</u>: If the result is an improper fraction, simplify it by converting it back to a mixed number.

Let's solve some problems:

$$1\frac{2}{4} \times 3\frac{1}{6} = \frac{3}{2} \times \frac{19}{6} = \frac{3 \times 19}{2 \times 6} = \frac{57}{12} = 4\frac{3}{4}$$

$1 \times 4 + 2 = 6 \;=\; \frac{6}{2} \;=\; \frac{3}{2} \qquad\qquad 3 \times 8 + 1 = \frac{19}{6}$

$$2\frac{6}{10} \div 6\frac{6}{7} = \frac{13}{5} \times \frac{7}{48} = \frac{13 \times 7}{5 \times 48} = \frac{91}{240}$$

$2 \times 10 + 6 = 26 \;=\; \frac{26}{10} \;=\; \frac{13}{5} \qquad\qquad 6 \times 7 + 6 = \frac{48}{7}$

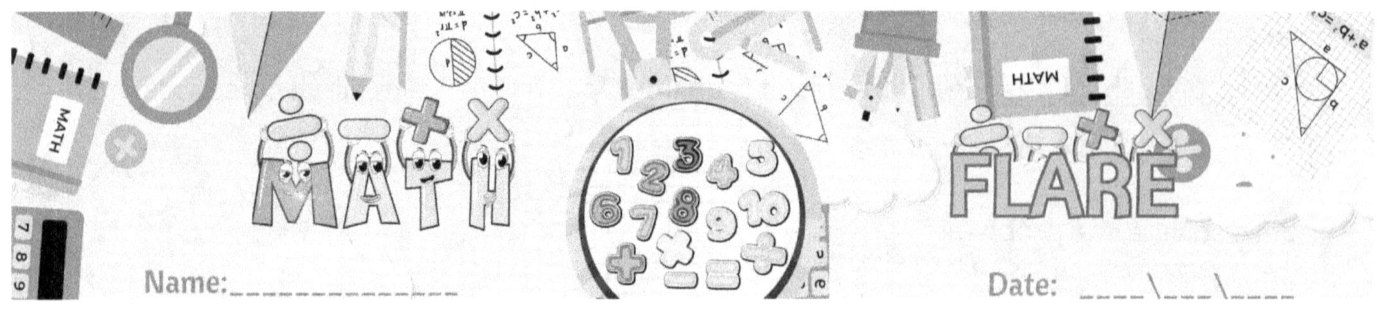

Name:_________________   Date: ______________

Adding Decimals

Find the sum.

1. 637.796 + 644.098	2. 632.666 + 462.142	3. 613.069 + 721.021	4. 617.160 + 964.611
5. 697.699 + 478.565	6. 497.284 + 768.818	7. 942.527 + 809.971	8. 692.379 + 643.300
9. 947.488 + 647.835	10. 339.942 + 537.538	11. 417.914 + 232.409	12. 375.387 + 439.376
13. 300.992 + 176.652	14. 677.547 + 864.643	15. 836.331 + 599.928	16. 523.840 + 534.722
17. 749.726 + 182.258	18. 818.310 + 515.260	19. 609.987 + 865.532	20. 796.554 + 482.578

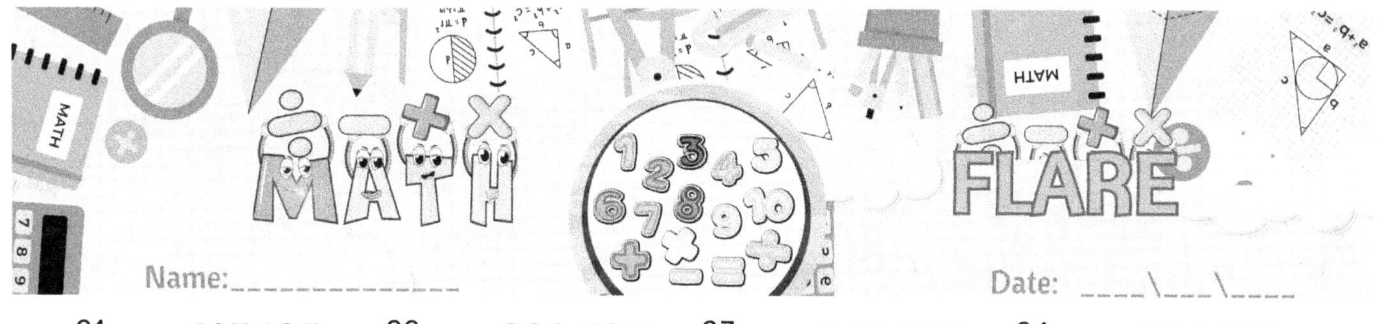

Name:_______________   Date: ____________

| 21. | 627.185
+ 219.125 | 22. | 992.703
+ 678.387 | 23. | 748.546
+ 756.520 | 24. | 791.133
+ 268.428 |

| 25. | 414.181
+ 336.743 | 26. | 419.175
+ 528.041 | 27. | 198.339
+ 792.759 | 28. | 744.738
+ 505.387 |

| 29. | 368.711
+ 293.291 | 30. | 261.150
+ 536.417 | 31. | 143.474
+ 752.516 | 32. | 228.280
+ 197.771 |

| 33. | 954.724
+ 962.561 | 34. | 119.092
+ 860.269 | 35. | 991.660
+ 277.119 | 36. | 133.314
+ 181.957 |

| 37. | 851.280
+ 857.363 | 38. | 910.352
+ 298.789 | 39. | 239.705
+ 696.998 | 40. | 690.829
+ 544.471 |

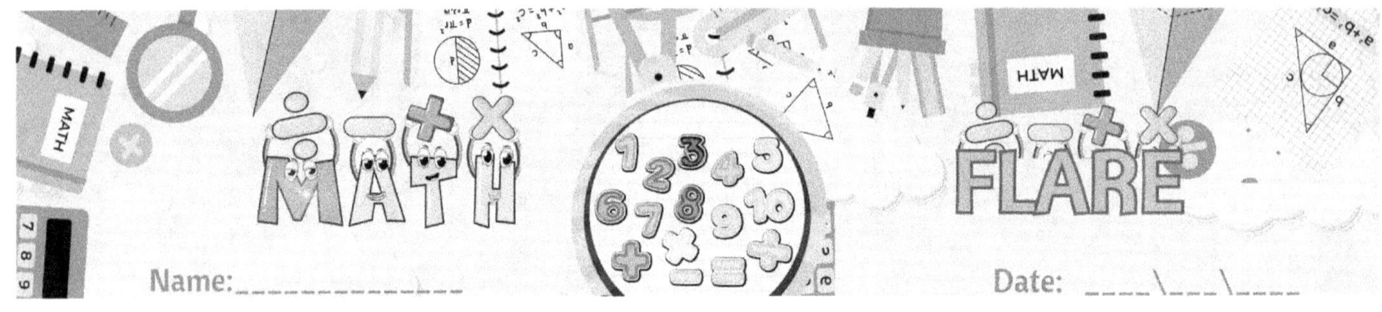

Subtracting Decimals

Find the difference.

41.	42.	43.	44.
902.381	481.907	463.068	366.858
− 489.830	− 713.448	− 845.713	− 308.578

45.	46.	47.	48.
745.039	946.541	306.909	183.888
− 231.726	− 734.258	− 809.276	− 333.400

49.	50.	51.	52.
372.691	653.561	876.459	178.069
− 327.814	− 126.327	− 216.607	− 412.961

53.	54.	55.	56.
502.746	229.624	224.851	687.737
− 783.893	− 104.429	− 728.971	− 876.852

57.	58.	59.	60.
966.532	684.429	703.708	483.655
− 650.703	− 469.739	− 209.195	− 492.179

61. 754.052 − 489.738	62. 952.576 − 777.828	63. 849.702 − 667.623	64. 681.743 − 523.140
65. 889.596 − 406.432	66. 258.080 − 759.662	67. 977.619 − 605.116	68. 679.273 − 785.694
69. 411.800 − 168.908	70. 310.763 − 679.047	71. 716.164 − 362.402	72. 183.748 − 116.003
73. 544.002 − 169.605	74. 767.788 − 656.094	75. 224.918 − 714.049	76. 629.714 − 263.469
77. 844.181 − 261.327	78. 372.277 − 486.643	79. 264.042 − 400.142	80. 563.289 − 834.992

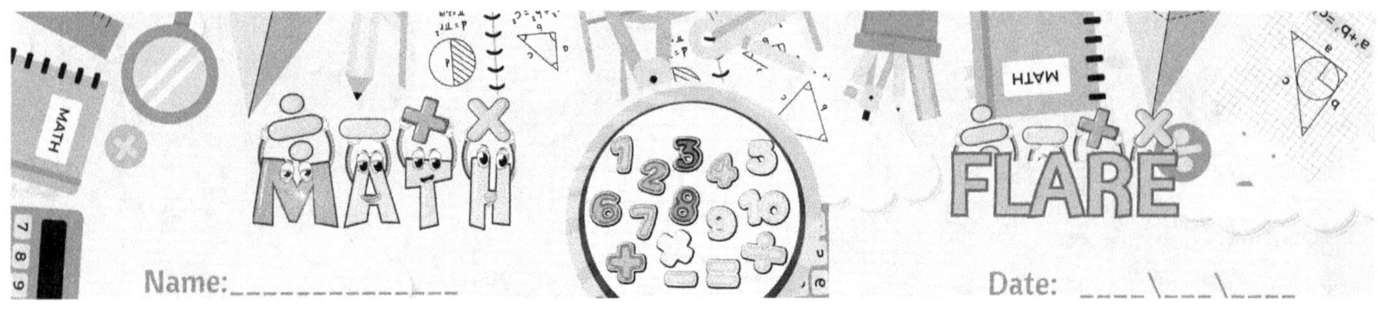

Name:____________________   Date: _______________

Multiplying Decimals
Find the product.

81.
$$85.62 \times 3.14$$

82.
$$79.87 \times 3.48$$

83.
$$36.50 \times 3.14$$

84.
$$40.17 \times 7.95$$

85.
$$36.24 \times 8.45$$

86.
$$72.50 \times 5.04$$

87.
$$51.25 \times 7.36$$

88.
$$33.04 \times 9.78$$

89.
$$84.82 \times 4.52$$

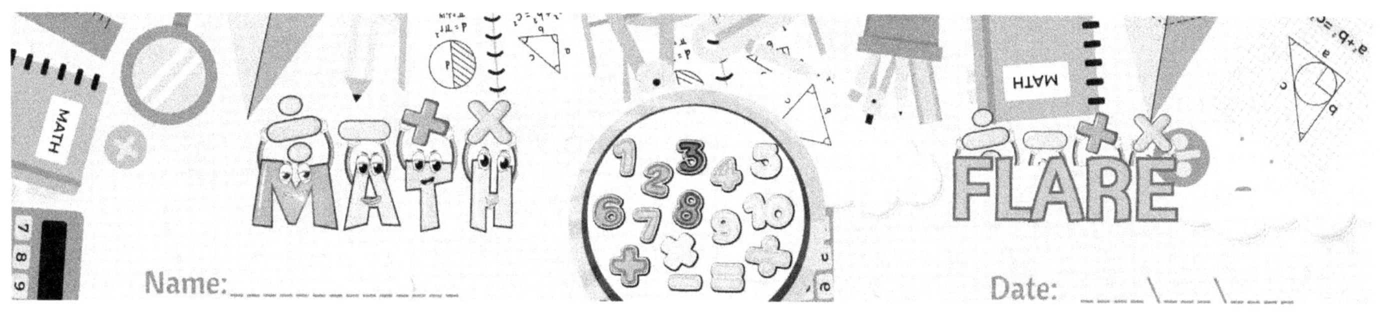

90. 11.75
   × 3.56

91. 99.43
   × 7.65

92. 69.09
   × 6.90

93. 93.50
   × 2.87

94. 12.13
   × 6.77

95. 74.72
   × 1.24

96. 18.90
   × 3.89

97. 23.03
   × 4.98

98. 36.28
   × 2.29

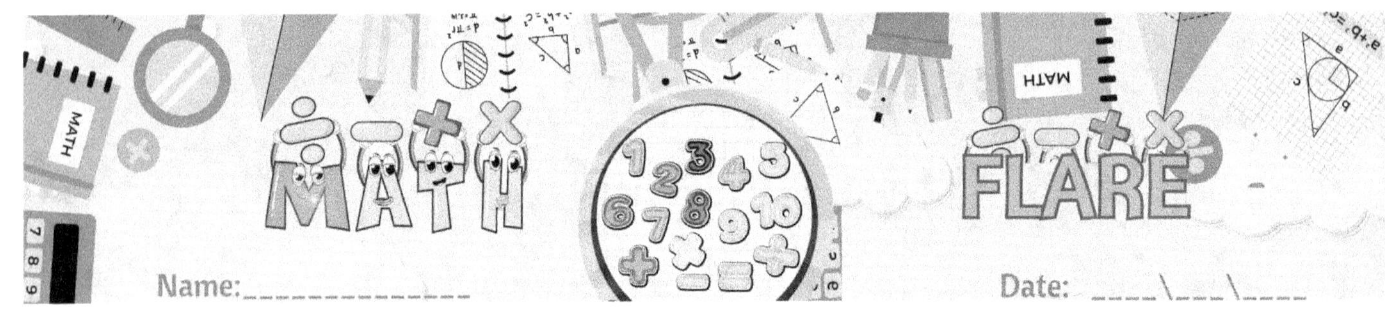

99.	47.50 × 1.35	100.	52.11 × 6.57	101.	62.44 × 4.61
102.	25.78 × 7.93	103.	11.60 × 2.82	104.	10.37 × 2.20
105.	66.61 × 5.78	106.	38.66 × 3.03	107.	81.81 × 5.25

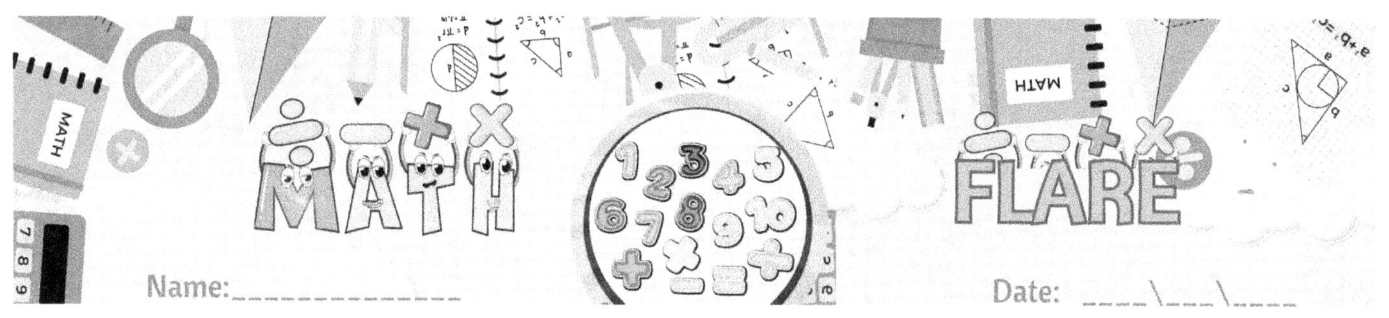

108. 46.02
    × 1.91
    ————

109. 62.32
    × 2.08
    ————

110. 41.34
    × 1.78
    ————

111. 29.31
    × 7.24
    ————

112. 14.88
    × 3.39
    ————

113. 75.70
    × 4.35
    ————

114. 37.39
    × 1.14
    ————

115. 47.35
    × 2.01
    ————

116. 60.41
    × 8.12
    ————

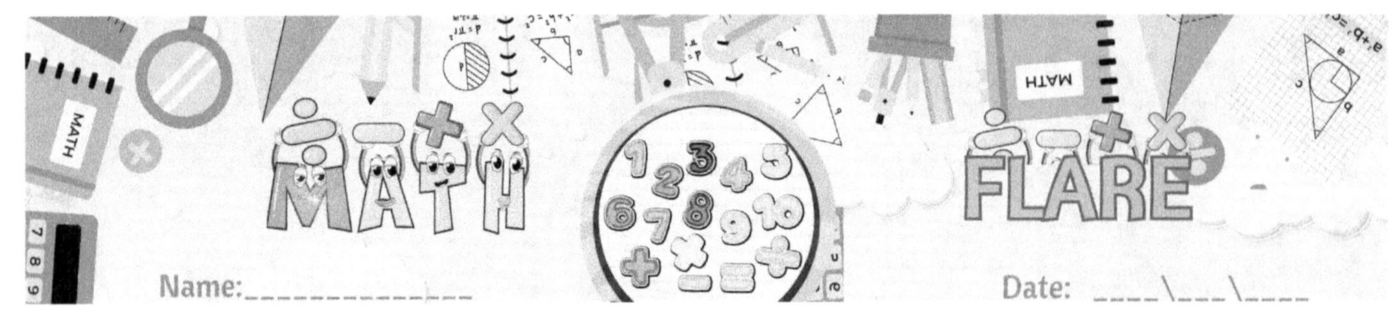

117.
$$\begin{array}{r} 93.12 \\ \times\ \ 4.60 \\ \hline \end{array}$$

118.
$$\begin{array}{r} 73.21 \\ \times\ \ 6.32 \\ \hline \end{array}$$

119.
$$\begin{array}{r} 60.76 \\ \times\ \ 8.97 \\ \hline \end{array}$$

120.
$$\begin{array}{r} 67.51 \\ \times\ \ 7.52 \\ \hline \end{array}$$

121.
$$\begin{array}{r} 28.37 \\ \times\ \ 9.01 \\ \hline \end{array}$$

122.
$$\begin{array}{r} 11.12 \\ \times\ \ 2.69 \\ \hline \end{array}$$

123.
$$\begin{array}{r} 73.69 \\ \times\ \ 8.85 \\ \hline \end{array}$$

124.
$$\begin{array}{r} 57.10 \\ \times\ \ 7.04 \\ \hline \end{array}$$

125.
$$\begin{array}{r} 13.78 \\ \times\ \ 2.72 \\ \hline \end{array}$$

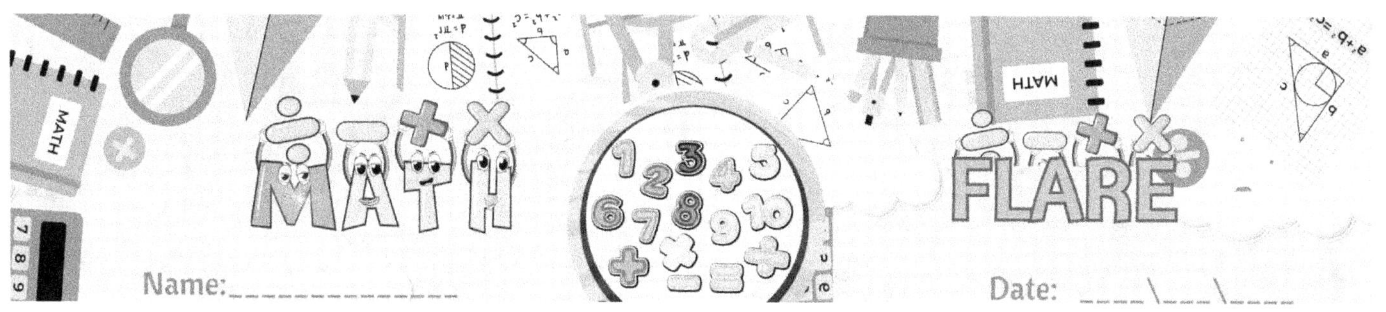

Dividing Decimals

Find the quotient.

126.

$$8\overline{)16.5}$$

127.

$$6\overline{)85.6}$$

128.

$$3\overline{)29.7}$$

129.

$$4\overline{)97.2}$$

130.

$$3\overline{)15.5}$$

131.

$$7\overline{)75.2}$$

132.

$$2\overline{)66.1}$$

133.

$$6\overline{)76.1}$$

134.

$$8\overline{)75.5}$$

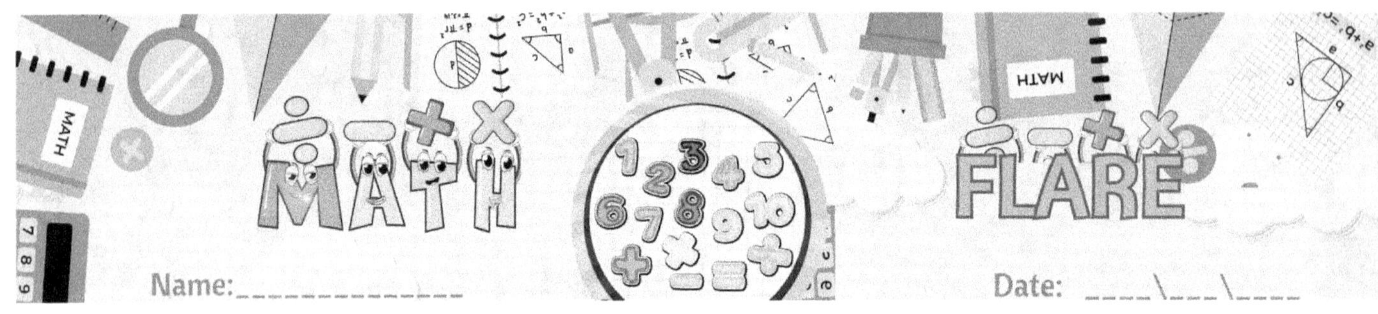

135.

$$9\overline{)10.0}$$

136.

$$9\overline{)46.8}$$

137.

$$8\overline{)84.1}$$

138.

$$10\overline{)76.4}$$

139.

$$2\overline{)81.6}$$

140.

$$4\overline{)13.3}$$

141.

$$1\overline{)60.5}$$

142.

$$8\overline{)56.7}$$

143.

$$9\overline{)16.6}$$

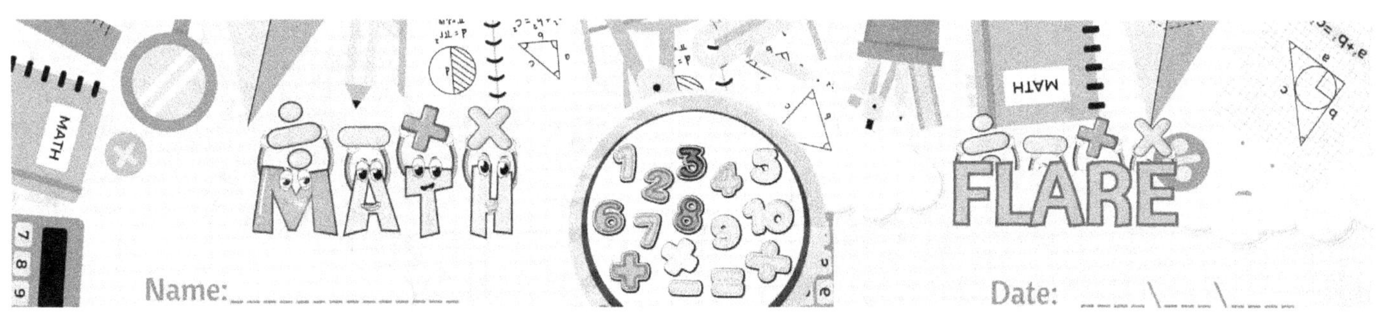

144.

$$10\overline{)70.0}$$

145.

$$7\overline{)59.2}$$

146.

$$2\overline{)35.6}$$

147.

$$9\overline{)18.7}$$

148.

$$2\overline{)82.9}$$

149.

$$8\overline{)81.0}$$

150.

$$4\overline{)13.6}$$

151.

$$7\overline{)28.1}$$

152.

$$3\overline{)48.3}$$

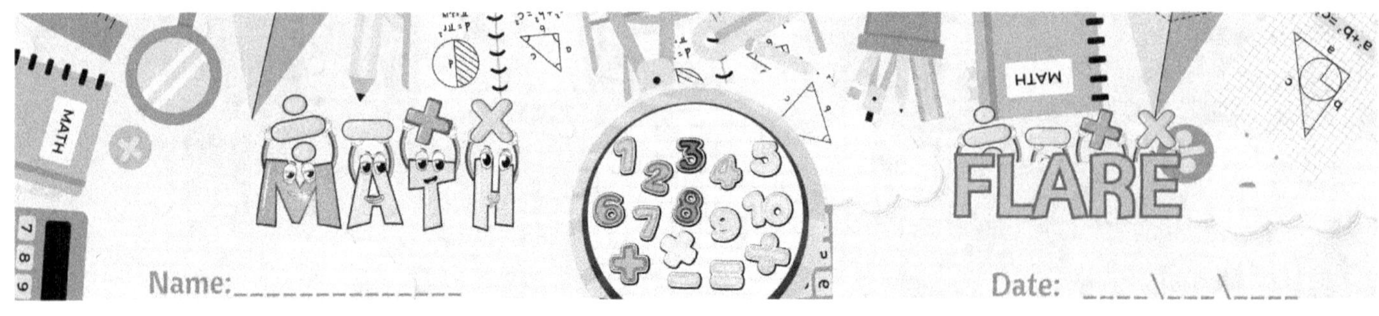

153.

$1\overline{)91.1}$

154.

$3\overline{)81.0}$

155.

$9\overline{)50.0}$

156.

$8\overline{)37.7}$

157.

$8\overline{)74.0}$

158.

$9\overline{)19.7}$

159.

$8\overline{)12.6}$

160.

$8\overline{)92.5}$

161.

$4\overline{)35.2}$

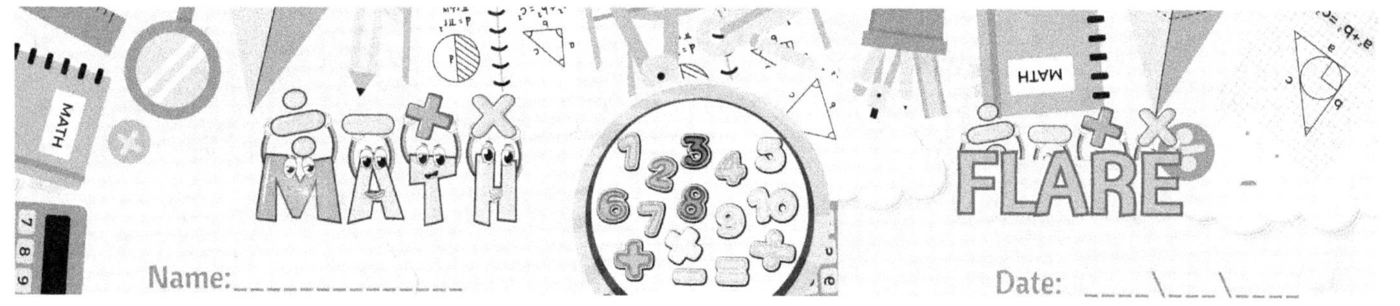

Fractions Multiplication

Find the product.

162. $\dfrac{15}{16} \times \dfrac{2}{15} =$ _______________

163. $\dfrac{1}{6} \times \dfrac{1}{10} =$ _______________

164. $\dfrac{12}{19} \times \dfrac{1}{19} =$ _______________

165. $\dfrac{9}{11} \times \dfrac{2}{3} =$ _______________

166. $\dfrac{13}{15} \times \dfrac{7}{8} =$ _______________

167. $\dfrac{3}{4} \times \dfrac{1}{2} =$ _______________

168. $\dfrac{1}{9} \times \dfrac{2}{3} =$ _______________

169. $\dfrac{1}{7} \times \dfrac{9}{10} =$ _______________

170. $\dfrac{1}{10} \times \dfrac{1}{2} =$ _______________

171. $\dfrac{16}{17} \times \dfrac{5}{6} =$ _______________

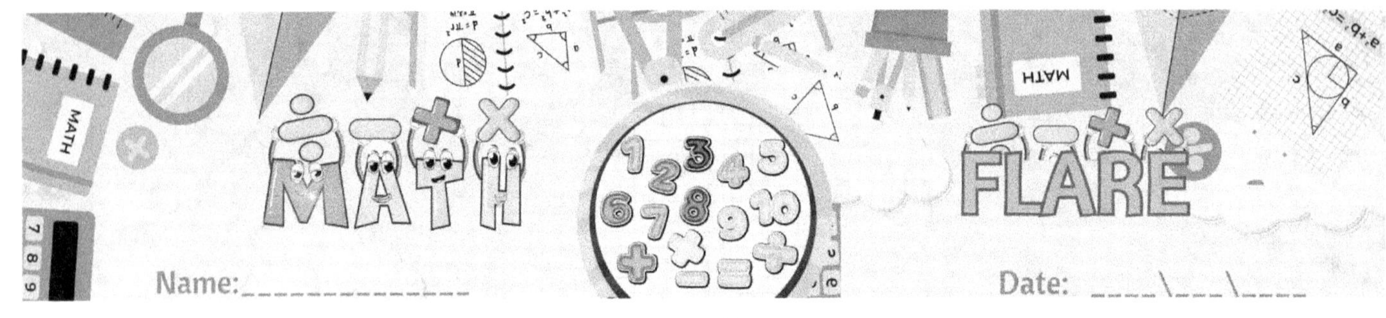

172. $\dfrac{7}{8} \times \dfrac{1}{3} =$ _______________

173. $\dfrac{4}{5} \times \dfrac{5}{7} =$ _______________

174. $\dfrac{13}{19} \times \dfrac{4}{5} =$ _______________

175. $\dfrac{1}{2} \times \dfrac{8}{13} =$ _______________

176. $\dfrac{1}{6} \times \dfrac{1}{4} =$ _______________

177. $\dfrac{2}{3} \times \dfrac{5}{6} =$ _______________

178. $\dfrac{7}{9} \times \dfrac{10}{11} =$ _______________

179. $\dfrac{4}{5} \times \dfrac{2}{5} =$ _______________

180. $\dfrac{1}{3} \times \dfrac{5}{9} =$ _______________

181. $\dfrac{8}{11} \times \dfrac{4}{5} =$ _______________

182. $\dfrac{3}{4} \times \dfrac{4}{13} =$ _______________

183. $\dfrac{1}{3} \times \dfrac{1}{2} =$ _______________

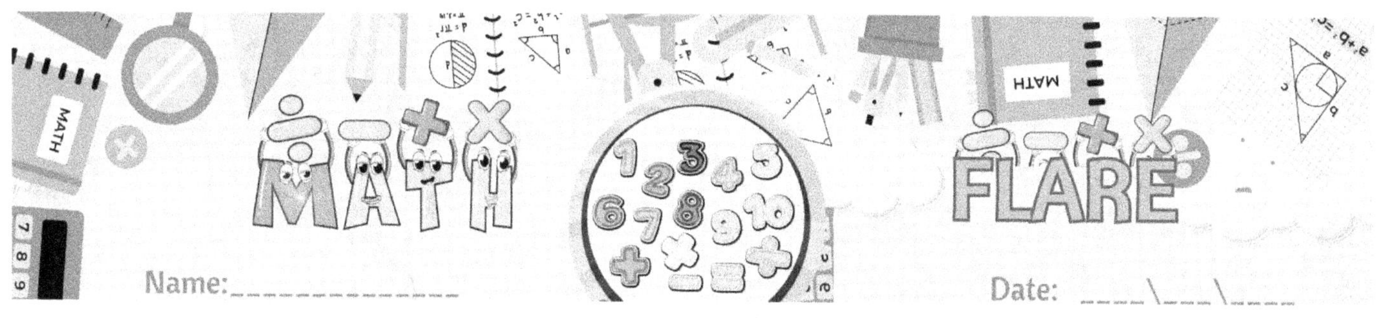

184. $\dfrac{1}{2} \times \dfrac{1}{17} =$ _______________

185. $\dfrac{1}{6} \times \dfrac{2}{3} =$ _______________

186. $\dfrac{2}{17} \times \dfrac{6}{7} =$ _______________

187. $\dfrac{5}{6} \times \dfrac{1}{4} =$ _______________

188. $\dfrac{6}{13} \times \dfrac{6}{11} =$ _______________

189. $\dfrac{1}{10} \times \dfrac{7}{12} =$ _______________

190. $\dfrac{6}{19} \times \dfrac{1}{2} =$ _______________

191. $\dfrac{1}{3} \times \dfrac{17}{20} =$ _______________

192. $\dfrac{11}{18} \times \dfrac{1}{3} =$ _______________

193. $\dfrac{1}{2} \times \dfrac{3}{4} =$ _______________

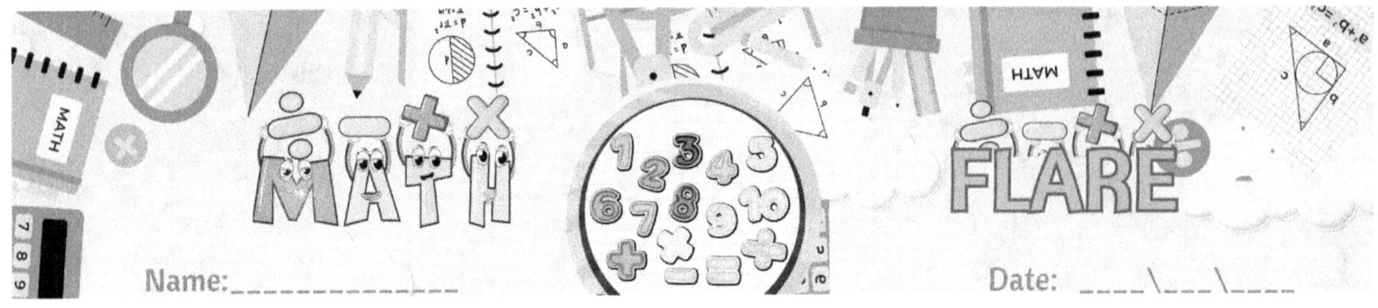

Name:______________________   Date: _______________

Fractions Division

Find the quotient.

194. $\dfrac{1}{13} \div \dfrac{3}{4} =$ _______________

195. $\dfrac{4}{7} \div \dfrac{1}{7} =$ _______________

196. $\dfrac{11}{16} \div \dfrac{9}{13} =$ _______________

197. $\dfrac{1}{4} \div \dfrac{1}{2} =$ _______________

198. $\dfrac{1}{6} \div \dfrac{13}{14} =$ _______________

199. $\dfrac{3}{13} \div \dfrac{6}{10} =$ _______________

200. $\dfrac{2}{19} \div \dfrac{1}{2} =$ _______________

201. $\dfrac{1}{15} \div \dfrac{11}{17} =$ _______________

202. $\dfrac{2}{3} \div \dfrac{9}{13} =$ _______________

203. $\dfrac{1}{2} \div \dfrac{3}{12} =$ _______________

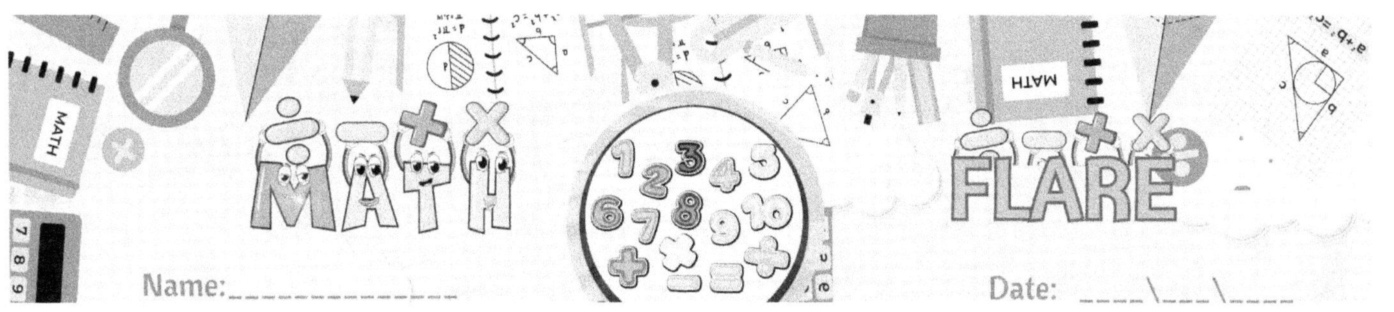

204. $\dfrac{1}{10} \div \dfrac{2}{4} =$ _______________

205. $\dfrac{5}{14} \div \dfrac{6}{18} =$ _______________

206. $\dfrac{15}{17} \div \dfrac{2}{7} =$ _______________

207. $\dfrac{1}{9} \div \dfrac{1}{15} =$ _______________

208. $\dfrac{1}{18} \div \dfrac{4}{5} =$ _______________

209. $\dfrac{2}{5} \div \dfrac{9}{20} =$ _______________

210. $\dfrac{11}{18} \div \dfrac{5}{10} =$ _______________

211. $\dfrac{13}{17} \div \dfrac{11}{12} =$ _______________

212. $\dfrac{8}{19} \div \dfrac{1}{19} =$ _______________

213. $\dfrac{4}{5} \div \dfrac{3}{8} =$ _______________

214. $\dfrac{3}{14} \div \dfrac{1}{3} =$ _______________

215. $\dfrac{1}{18} \div \dfrac{8}{16} =$ _______________

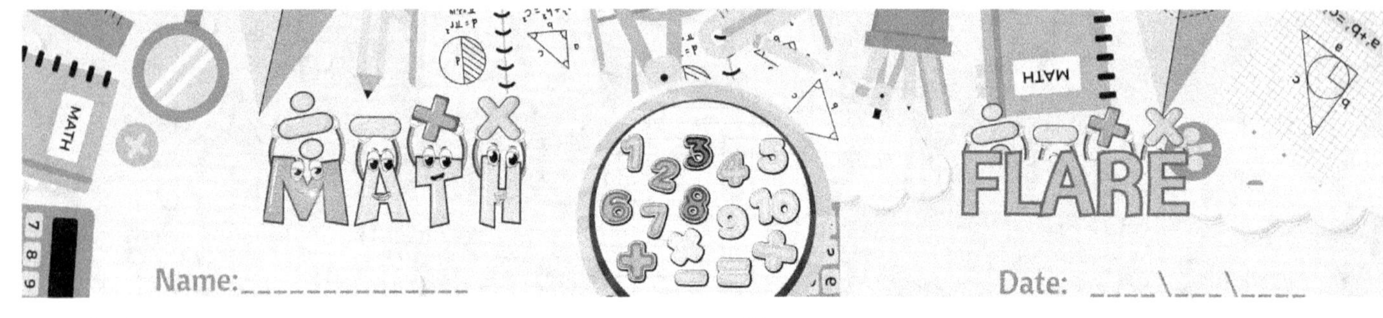

Name:________________   Date: ____________

216. $\dfrac{4}{15} \div \dfrac{5}{12} =$ _______________

217. $\dfrac{2}{3} \div \dfrac{7}{19} =$ _______________

218. $\dfrac{3}{8} \div \dfrac{12}{18} =$ _______________

219. $\dfrac{1}{12} \div \dfrac{14}{17} =$ _______________

220. $\dfrac{8}{11} \div \dfrac{5}{11} =$ _______________

221. $\dfrac{4}{7} \div \dfrac{1}{2} =$ _______________

222. $\dfrac{2}{9} \div \dfrac{5}{19} =$ _______________

223. $\dfrac{1}{18} \div \dfrac{4}{7} =$ _______________

224. $\dfrac{13}{19} \div \dfrac{9}{16} =$ _______________

225. $\dfrac{3}{8} \div \dfrac{4}{12} =$ _______________

Fractions Multiplication Word Problems

226. Aiden is baking a cake that requires $\frac{4}{10}$ cup of flour. If he wants to make 4 times as much cake , how much flour does he need?

227. If a recipe calls for $\frac{2}{6}$ cup of butter and you want to make $\frac{2}{5}$ as much, how much butter do you need?

228. If a container holds $\frac{2}{4}$ of a gallon of water and you need 3 gallons of water, how many containers do you need?

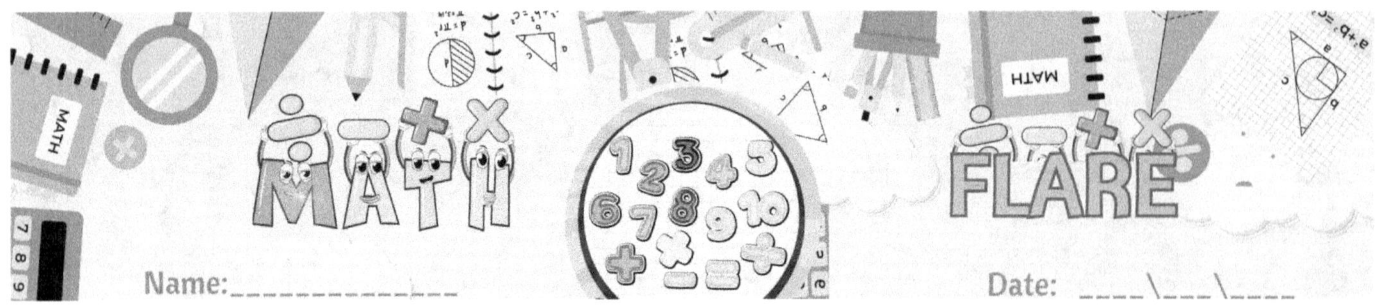

Name:_______________ Date: ____________

229. A factory can produce $\frac{7}{8}$ of a car in one hour. How many cars can the factory produce in 8 hours?

230. A basketball team wins $\frac{1}{2}$ of their games. If they play 10 games in a season, how many games did they win?

231. If a person can run at a speed of $\frac{4}{6}$ miles per hour, how long will it take him to run 4 miles?

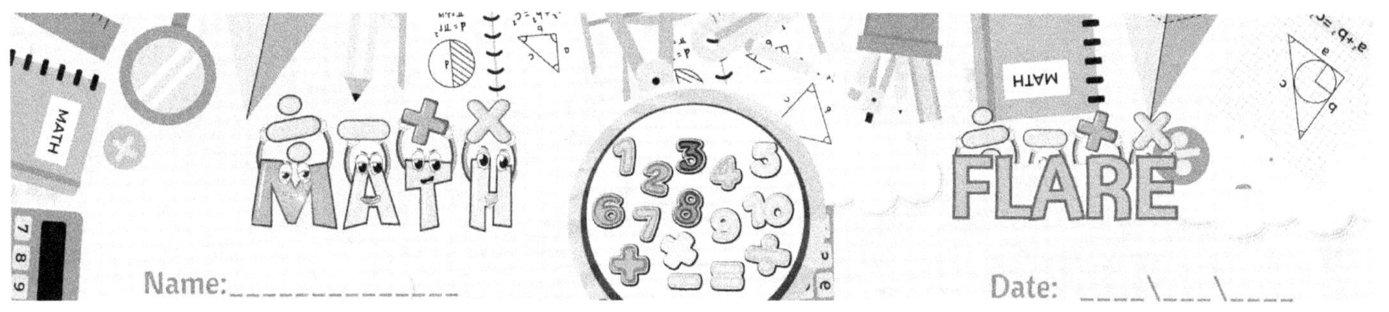

232. Ryan spent $\frac{1}{4}$ of his money to buy shirts. His friend Aaron spent 3 times more to buy the shirts. How much did Aaron spend?

233. If a cake recipe calls for $\frac{4}{10}$ cup of flour and you want to make 4 cakes, how much flour do you need?

234. Harper drove $\frac{1}{3}$ of the distance to the mall. If the distance to the mall is $\frac{3}{4}$ miles, how far did Harper drive?

235. If a garden has an area of $\frac{5}{6}$ square feet and you want to increase it by a factor of 2, what will be the new area of the garden?

236. If a car can travel $\frac{1}{9}$ of a mile on one gallon of gas, how many miles can it travel on 3 gallons of gas?

237. If a container holds $\frac{1}{5}$ of a bags of scalpels and you need 3 bags of scalpels, how many containers do you need?

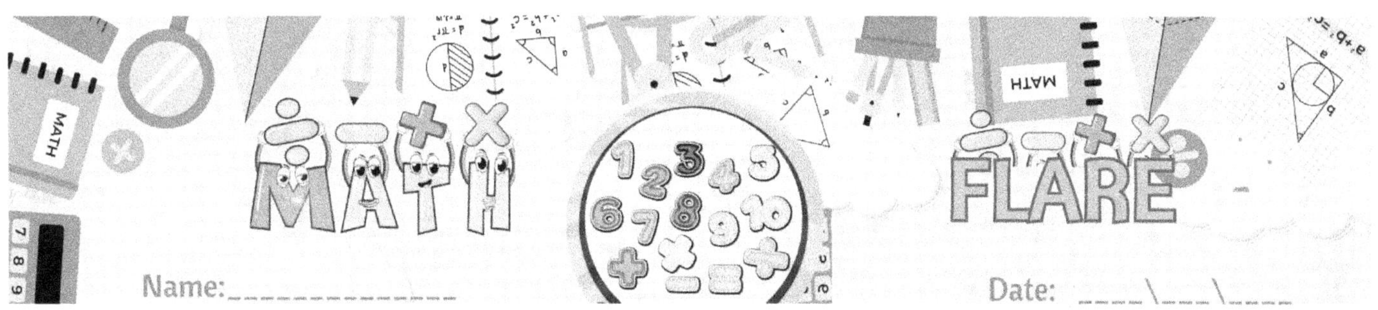

238. Caroline ran $\frac{1}{2}$ miles every day for 10 days. How many miles did she run in total?

239. If a company can produce $\frac{6}{9}$ of a product in one day, how many days will it take to produce 4 products?

240. A cake recipe calls for $\frac{7}{8}$ cups of sugar to make one cake. If Riley wants to make 6 cakes, how many cups of sugar will she need?

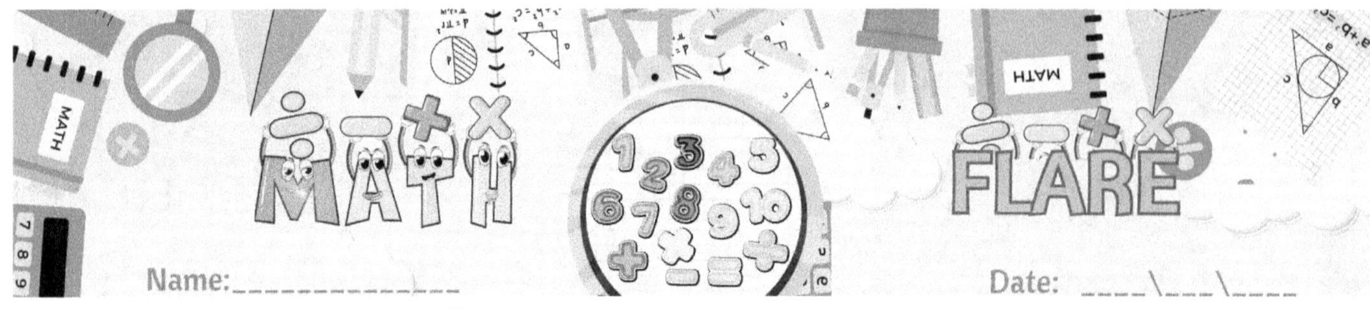

241. Cameron needs $\frac{5}{6}$ cup of flour for a recipe and he wants to make $\frac{8}{10}$ batches of the recipe, how much flour will he need in total?

242. If you need to make 5 batches of cookies, and each batch requires $\frac{1}{3}$ cup of chocolate chips, how many cups of chocolate chips do you need in total?

243. Nolan is making a dish that calls for $\frac{2}{6}$ cup of cooking oil. If he wants to make 2 dishes of the same recipe, how much cooking oil does he need?

244. If a recipe calls for $\frac{2}{4}$ cup of flour and you want to make it 5, how much flour do you need?

245. A bike tire has a radius of $\frac{9}{10}$ foot. If the tire rolls 6 times, how far does the bike travel?

246. If a bag of flour weighs $\frac{2}{4}$ of a pound and you need $\frac{7}{8}$ bags, how many pounds of flour do you need in total?

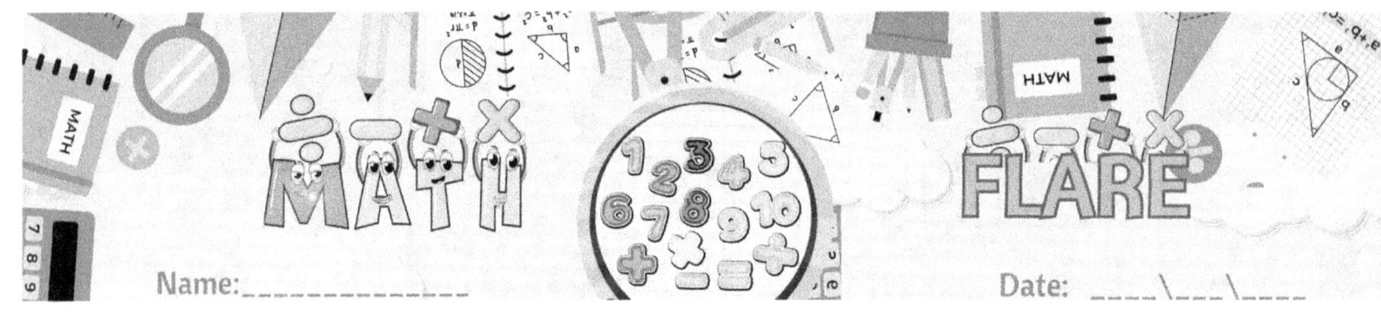

Fractions Division Word Problems

247. If you have $\frac{1}{8}$ of a cake and you want to divide it equally among 5 people, what fraction of the cake will each person get?

248. If a bottle contains $\frac{5}{7}$ of a liter of juice and you want to split it equally between 3 people, how much juice will each person get?

249. If you have $\frac{2}{3}$ of a pie and you want to share it equally with 3 friends, what fraction of the pie will each friend get?

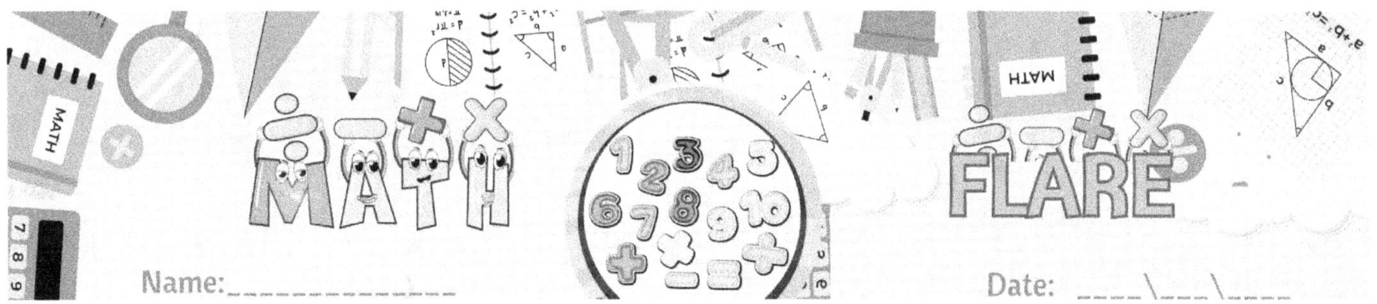

250. If you divide $\frac{1}{5}$ by $\frac{4}{5}$, what is the answer?

251. If you have $\frac{5}{9}$ of a cup of sugar and you want to divide it equally into 2 bowls, what fraction of a cup of sugar will each bowl get?

252. If a farmer has $\frac{1}{10}$ of an acre of land to plant corn, and he wants to divide the land equally into 3 parts, how much land will each part have?

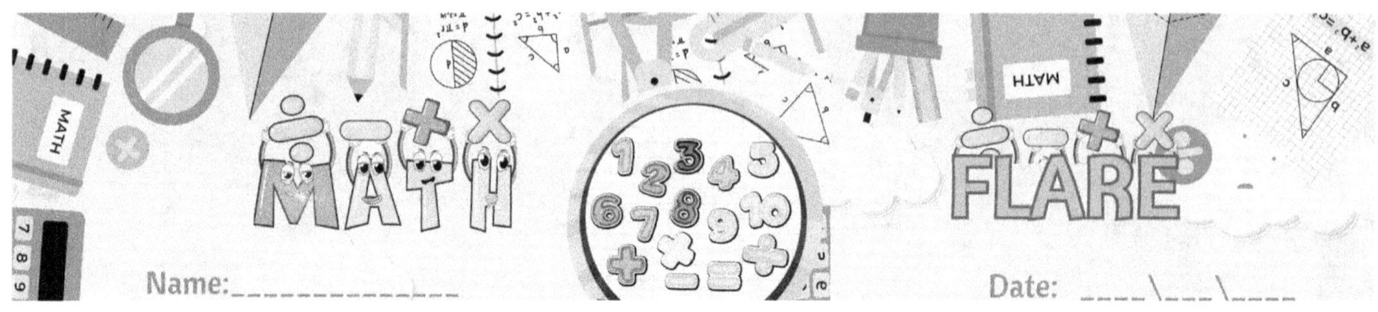

Date: ____________

253. Levi has $\frac{2}{4}$ of a cup of juice and he wants to divide it equally into 5 cups, what fraction of a cup of juice will each cup get?

254. If you have $\frac{4}{8}$ of a gallon of water and you want to divide it equally among 2 jugs, what fraction of a gallon of water will each jug get?

255. Emily has $\frac{5}{6}$ of a bag of maps and she wants to divide it equally among 3 people, what fraction of the bag of maps will each person get?

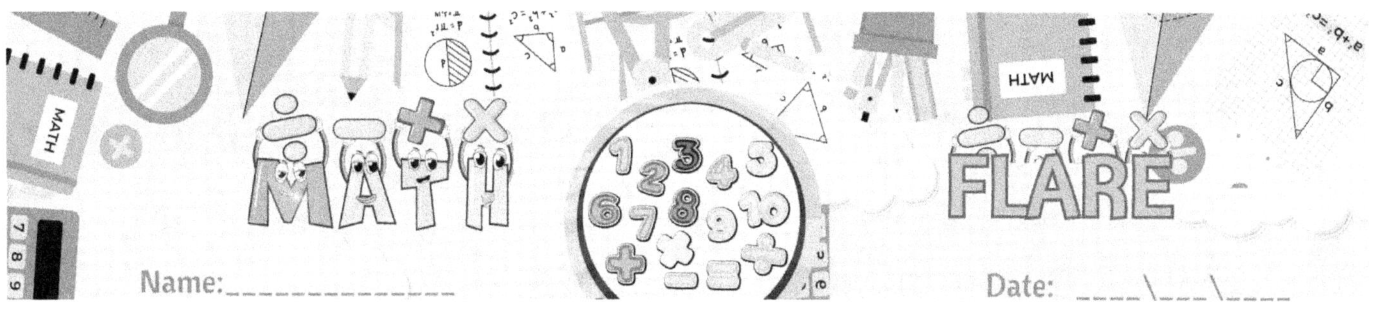

256. If you have $\frac{1}{2}$ of a pizza and you want to share it equally with 4 friends, what fraction of the pizza will each friend get?

257. Brielle has $\frac{2}{4}$ of a pound of beef and she wants to divide it equally among 3 burgers, what fraction of a pound of beef will each burger get?

258. If you have $\frac{2}{3}$ of a pound of ground beef and you want to make 6 patties, how much beef is needed for each patty?

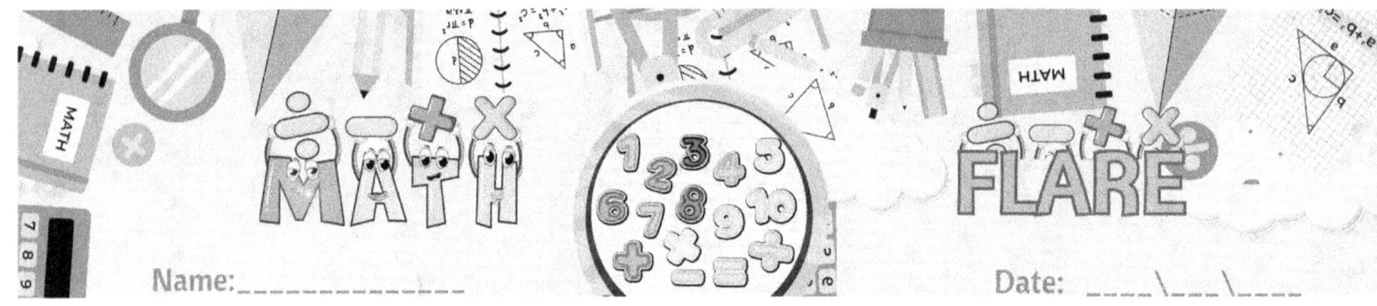

259. If you have $\frac{6}{7}$ of a pound of cheese and you want to divide it equally among 4 sandwiches, what fraction of a pound of cheese will each sandwich get?

260. If you have $\frac{6}{8}$ of a pie and you want to share it equally with 3 friends, what fraction of the pie will each friend get?

261. If you have $\frac{4}{9}$ of a cup of sugar and you want to divide it equally into 2 bowls, what fraction of a cup of sugar will each bowl get?

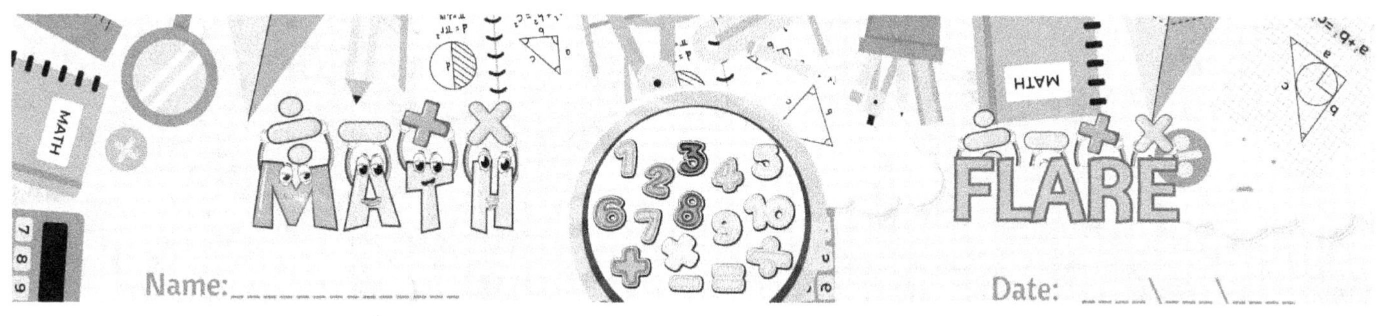

262. If you have $\frac{1}{2}$ of a gallon of water and you want to divide it equally among 2 jugs, what fraction of a gallon of water will each jug get?

263. Henry has $\frac{2}{6}$ of a cup of juice and he wants to divide it equally into 5 cups, what fraction of a cup of juice will each cup get?

264. Ava has $\frac{4}{5}$ of a bag of sticks and she wants to divide it equally among 3 people, what fraction of the bag of sticks will each person get?

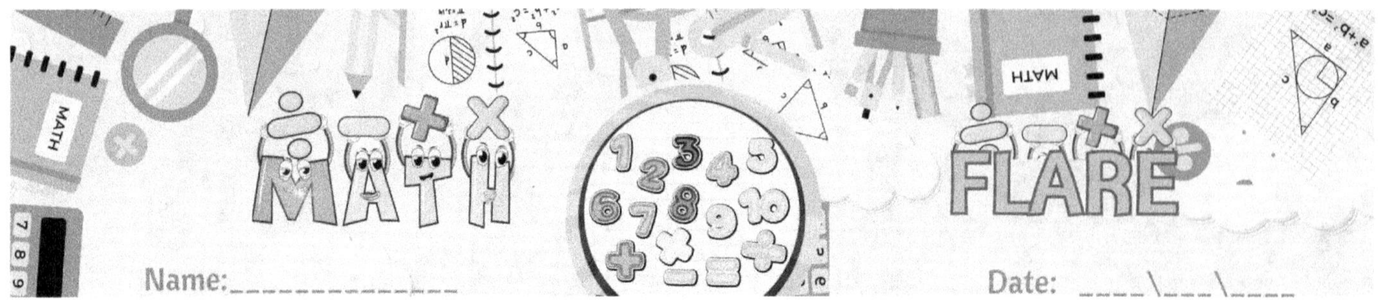

265. If you divide $\frac{8}{10}$ by $\frac{7}{10}$, what is the answer?

266. If you have $\frac{6}{8}$ of a cake and you want to divide it equally among 5 people, what fraction of the cake will each person get?

267. If a farmer has $\frac{5}{6}$ of an acre of land to plant corn, and he wants to divide the land equally into 3 parts, how much land will each part have?

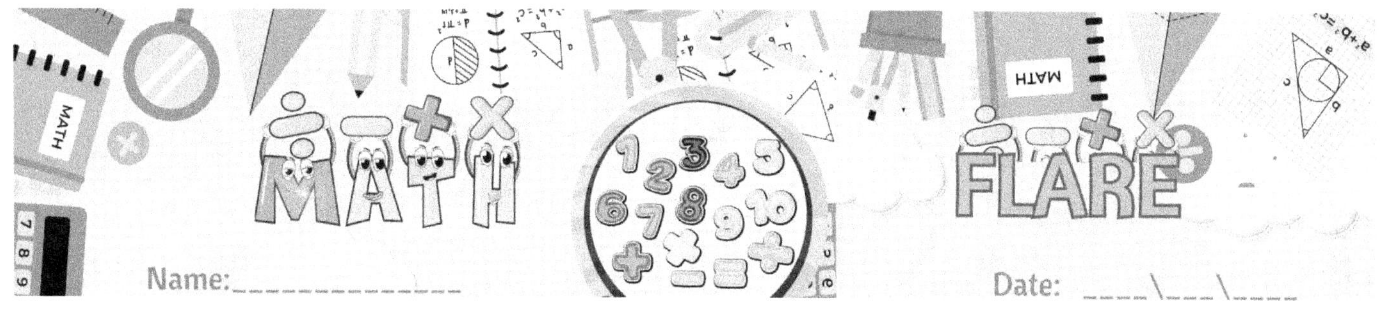

Convert Fractions and Decimals

268. $\dfrac{3}{8}$ = _______________

269. 0.4 = _______________

270. $\dfrac{11}{13}$ = _______________

271. 0.75 = _______________

272. 0.167 = _______________

273. $\dfrac{16}{20}$ = _______________

274. $\dfrac{7}{18}$ = _______________

275. 0.857 = _______________

276. $\dfrac{4}{5}$ = _______________

277. $\dfrac{2}{14}$ = _______________

278. $\dfrac{2}{9}$ = _______________

279. $\dfrac{4}{8}$ = _______________

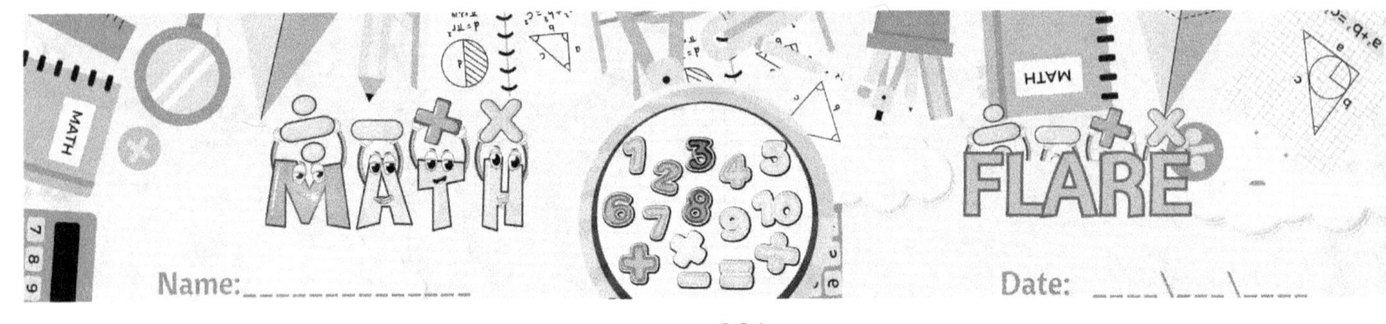

280. $0.706 =$ _______________

281. $\dfrac{6}{16} =$ _______________

282. $\dfrac{1}{3} =$ _______________

283. $0.5 =$ _______________

284. $\dfrac{4}{11} =$ _______________

285. $\dfrac{2}{12} =$ _______________

286. $\dfrac{14}{15} =$ _______________

287. $\dfrac{8}{19} =$ _______________

288. $0.3 =$ _______________

289. $0.6 =$ _______________

290. $0.333 =$ _______________

291. $0.875 =$ _______________

292. $0.062 =$ ______________

293. $0.167 =$ ______________

294. $\dfrac{4}{15} =$ ______________

295. $\dfrac{1}{4} =$ ______________

296. $0.786 =$ ______________

297. $\dfrac{4}{6} =$ ______________

298. $0.182 =$ ______________

299. $0.429 =$ ______________

300. $\dfrac{1}{17} =$ ______________

301. $0.385 =$ ______________

302. $\dfrac{13}{19} =$ ______________

303. $0.474 =$ ______________

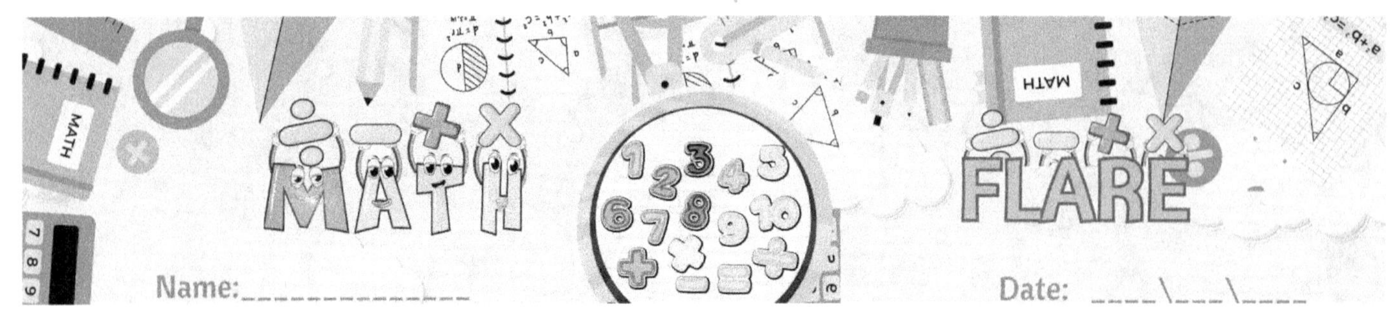

304. $0.714 =$ _______________

305. $0.556 =$ _______________

306. $\dfrac{14}{18} =$ _______________

307. $\dfrac{12}{16} =$ _______________

308. $\dfrac{5}{7} =$ _______________

309. $\dfrac{5}{11} =$ _______________

310. $0.529 =$ _______________

311. $0.615 =$ _______________

312. $0.2 =$ _______________

313. $\dfrac{2}{4} =$ _______________

314. $0.75 =$ _______________

315. $\dfrac{3}{5} =$ _______________

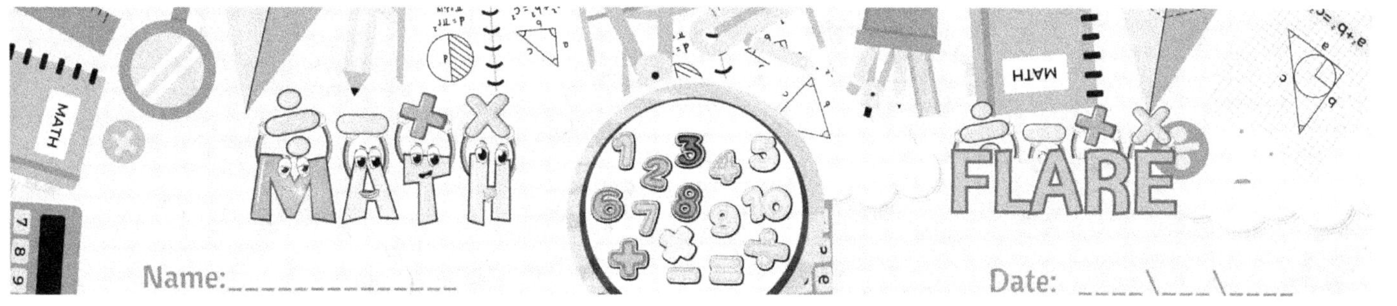

Mixed Numbers

Convert the Mixed numbers into improper fractions.

316. $6\frac{5}{12}$ = _______________

317. $6\frac{7}{9}$ = _______________

318. $4\frac{9}{10}$ = _______________

319. $3\frac{4}{9}$ = _______________

320. $3\frac{2}{4}$ = _______________

321. $7\frac{1}{8}$ = _______________

322. $7\frac{1}{2}$ = _______________

323. $5\frac{6}{12}$ = _______________

324. $4\frac{6}{8}$ = _______________

325. $2\frac{5}{18}$ = _______________

326. $1\frac{3}{10}$ = _______________

327. $1\frac{6}{7}$ = _______________

328. $8\frac{3}{4}$ = _______________

329. $7\frac{9}{12}$ = _______________

330. $1\frac{7}{9} =$ _______________

331. $8\frac{5}{6} =$ _______________

332. $3\frac{1}{7} =$ _______________

333. $1\frac{8}{20} =$ _______________

334. $6\frac{2}{4} =$ _______________

335. $1\frac{3}{9} =$ _______________

336. $1\frac{7}{12} =$ _______________

337. $5\frac{8}{14} =$ _______________

338. $4\frac{7}{8} =$ _______________

339. $8\frac{5}{14} =$ _______________

340. $3\frac{4}{8} =$ _______________

341. $5\frac{4}{10} =$ _______________

342. $4\frac{5}{18} =$ _______________

343. $7\frac{9}{20} =$ _______________

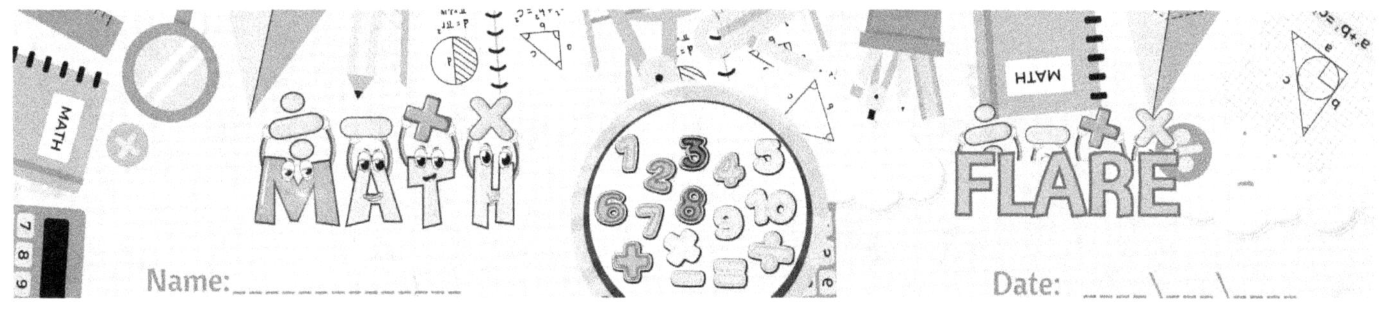

344. $1\frac{4}{8} =$ _______________

345. $7\frac{6}{12} =$ _______________

346. $6\frac{8}{9} =$ _______________

347. $2\frac{8}{18} =$ _______________

348. $7\frac{5}{8} =$ _______________

349. $9\frac{2}{10} =$ _______________

350. $8\frac{2}{3} =$ _______________

351. $7\frac{6}{7} =$ _______________

352. $2\frac{3}{7} =$ _______________

353. $8\frac{9}{18} =$ _______________

354. $6\frac{1}{2} =$ _______________

355. $9\frac{3}{8} =$ _______________

356. $1\frac{1}{3} =$ _______________

357. $4\frac{10}{12} =$ _______________

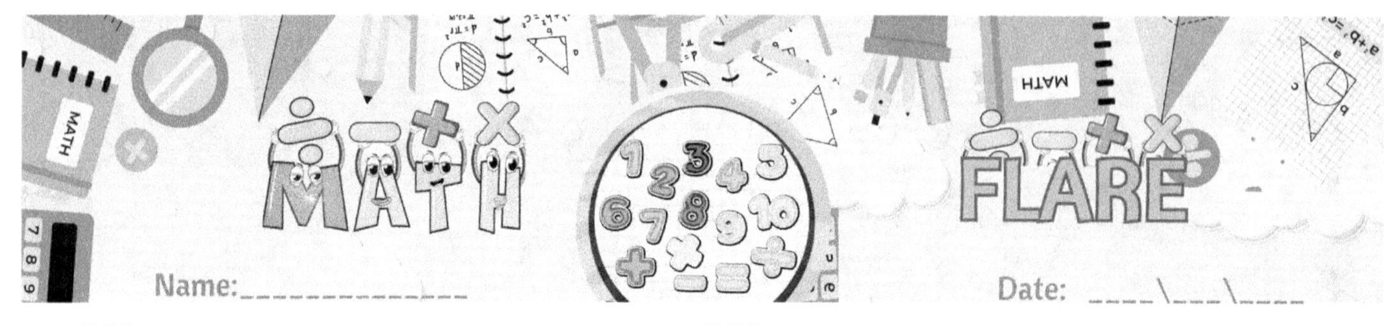

358. $6\frac{5}{6}$ = __________

359. $6\frac{4}{18}$ = __________

360. $5\frac{6}{10}$ = __________

361. $5\frac{5}{8}$ = __________

362. $9\frac{5}{9}$ = __________

363. $3\frac{1}{4}$ = __________

364. $4\frac{3}{6}$ = __________

365. $8\frac{6}{12}$ = __________

366. $7\frac{3}{5}$ = __________

367. $3\frac{7}{8}$ = __________

368. $4\frac{2}{8}$ = __________

369. $9\frac{2}{14}$ = __________

370. $5\frac{2}{6}$ = __________

371. $4\frac{6}{20}$ = __________

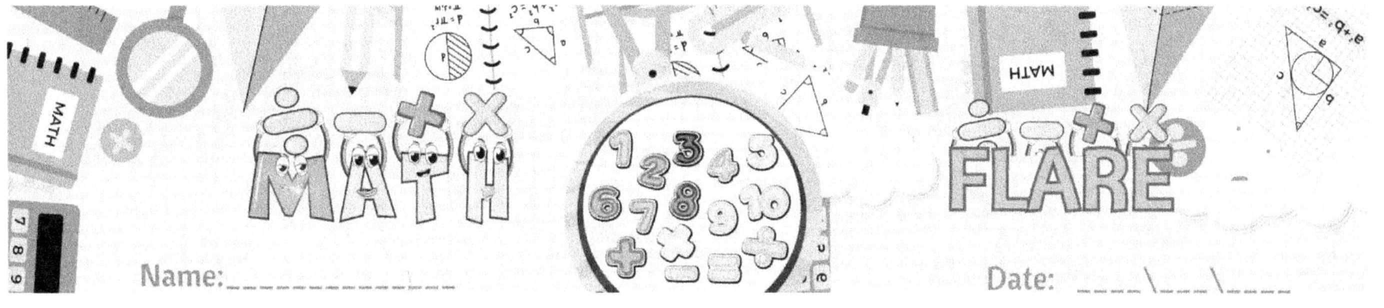

Mixed Numbers

Convert the Improper fractions into Mixed numbers.

372. $\dfrac{33}{7}$ = _______________

373. $\dfrac{12}{7}$ = _______________

374. $\dfrac{7}{6}$ = _______________

375. $\dfrac{57}{10}$ = _______________

376. $\dfrac{13}{4}$ = _______________

377. $\dfrac{71}{20}$ = _______________

378. $\dfrac{43}{8}$ = _______________

379. $\dfrac{19}{12}$ = _______________

380. $\dfrac{77}{10}$ = _______________

381. $\dfrac{67}{7}$ = _______________

382. $\dfrac{21}{4}$ = _______________

383. $\dfrac{27}{4}$ = _______________

384. $\dfrac{34}{5}$ = _______________

385. $\dfrac{44}{10}$ = _______________

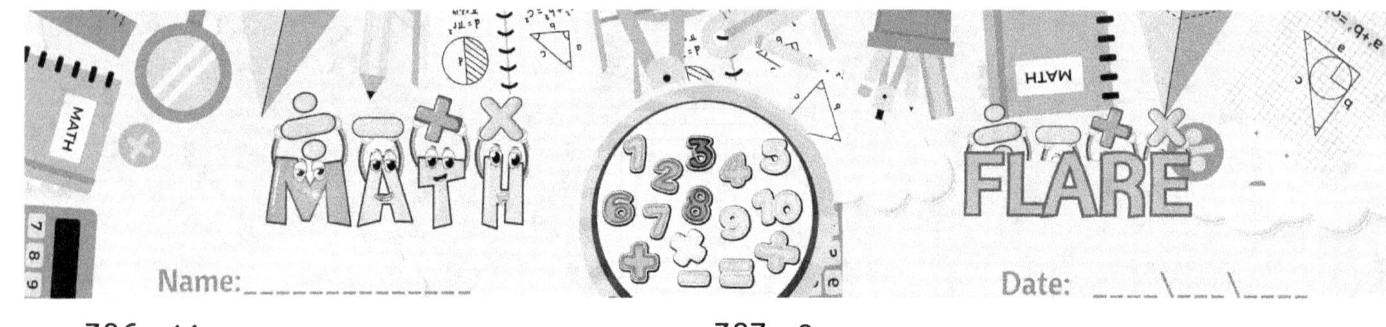

386. $\dfrac{14}{4}$ = _____________________

387. $\dfrac{8}{7}$ = _____________________

388. $\dfrac{16}{6}$ = _____________________

389. $\dfrac{32}{12}$ = _____________________

390. $\dfrac{170}{18}$ = _____________________

391. $\dfrac{18}{8}$ = _____________________

392. $\dfrac{22}{6}$ = _____________________

393. $\dfrac{36}{10}$ = _____________________

394. $\dfrac{83}{20}$ = _____________________

395. $\dfrac{23}{10}$ = _____________________

396. $\dfrac{86}{18}$ = _____________________

397. $\dfrac{29}{6}$ = _____________________

398. $\dfrac{17}{2}$ = _____________________

399. $\dfrac{36}{16}$ = _____________________

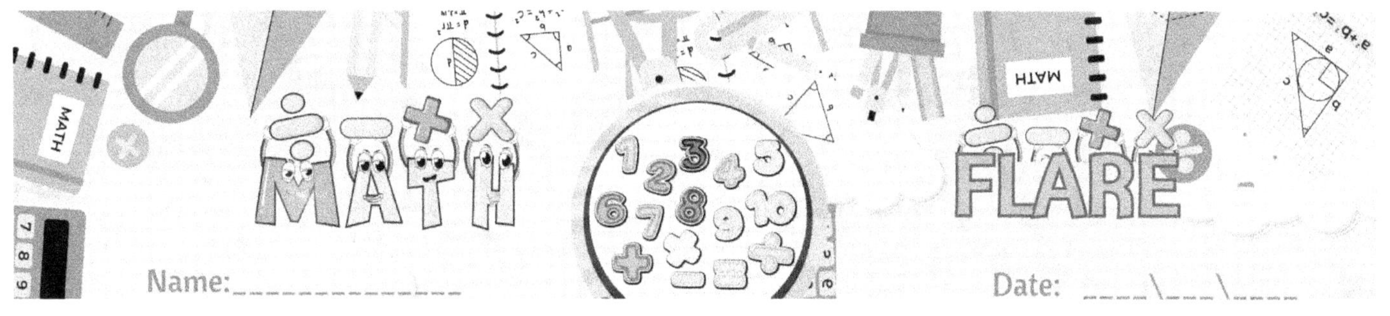

400. $\dfrac{143}{20}$ = _______________

401. $\dfrac{43}{9}$ = _______________

402. $\dfrac{17}{14}$ = _______________

403. $\dfrac{19}{4}$ = _______________

404. $\dfrac{11}{8}$ = _______________

405. $\dfrac{44}{6}$ = _______________

406. $\dfrac{20}{3}$ = _______________

407. $\dfrac{54}{10}$ = _______________

408. $\dfrac{127}{16}$ = _______________

409. $\dfrac{41}{7}$ = _______________

410. $\dfrac{26}{6}$ = _______________

411. $\dfrac{19}{9}$ = _______________

412. $\dfrac{56}{6}$ = _______________

413. $\dfrac{74}{10}$ = _______________

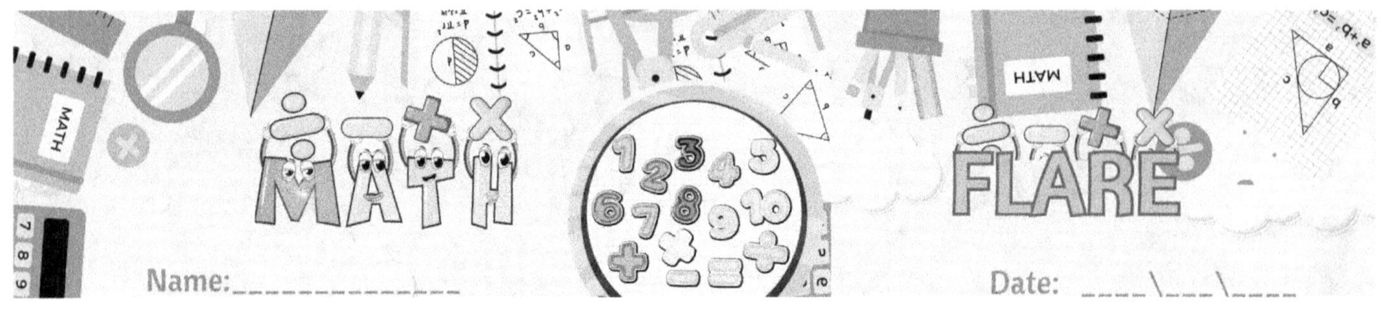

Name:_______________   Date: ____________

Mixed Numbers: Addition and Subtraction

Calculate.

414. $8\frac{4}{6} - 7\frac{4}{8} =$ _______________________________

415. $7\frac{5}{7} - 2\frac{2}{4} =$ _______________________________

416. $2\frac{1}{5} + 9\frac{1}{3} =$ _______________________________

417. $7\frac{1}{2} - 6\frac{2}{8} =$ _______________________________

418. $5\frac{1}{4} + 3\frac{2}{3} =$ _______________________________

419. $4\frac{6}{10} - 1\frac{3}{5} =$ _______________________________

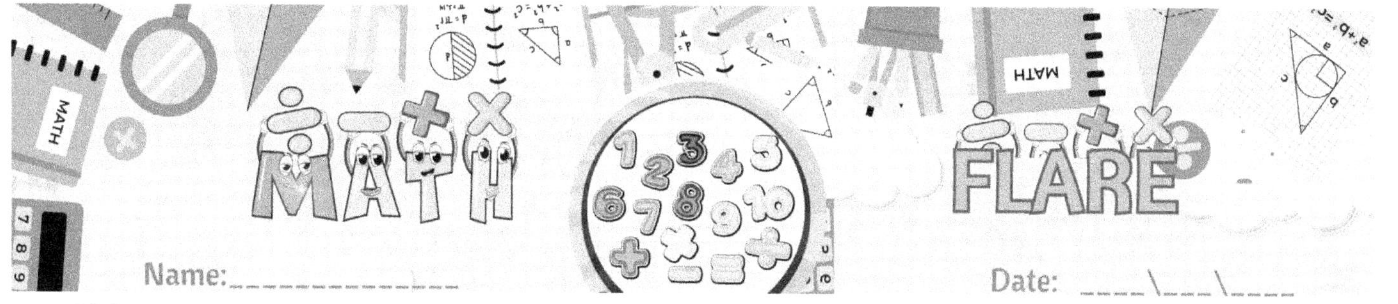

420. $2\frac{1}{2} + 2\frac{6}{7} =$ ________________________

421. $2\frac{4}{9} + 9\frac{2}{6} =$ ________________________

422. $5\frac{4}{5} + 2\frac{1}{6} =$ ________________________

423. $6\frac{1}{4} + 2\frac{1}{3} =$ ________________________

424. $5\frac{3}{7} + 9\frac{7}{8} =$ ________________________

425. $7\frac{2}{10} - 5\frac{3}{9} =$ ________________________

426. $7\frac{1}{2} - 3\frac{2}{3} =$ ___________________________

427. $5\frac{5}{7} + 9\frac{1}{2} =$ ___________________________

428. $8\frac{1}{6} - 1\frac{4}{8} =$ ___________________________

429. $8\frac{3}{4} + 7\frac{1}{10} =$ ___________________________

430. $7\frac{3}{9} - 6\frac{2}{5} =$ ___________________________

431. $2\frac{1}{6} + 9\frac{7}{9} =$ ___________________________

432. $6\frac{1}{3} - 3\frac{3}{4} =$ _______________

433. $7\frac{7}{10} + 1\frac{6}{7} =$ _______________

434. $7\frac{1}{2} - 5\frac{3}{8} =$ _______________

435. $7\frac{2}{5} + 8\frac{5}{10} =$ _______________

436. $6\frac{6}{9} + 9\frac{1}{2} =$ _______________

437. $8\frac{5}{7} - 7\frac{2}{3} =$ _______________

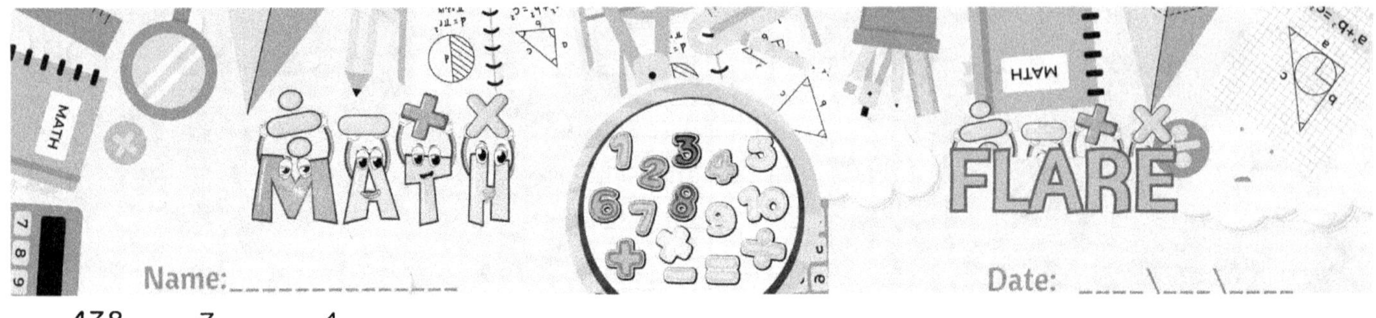

438. $4\frac{3}{6} + 3\frac{1}{5} =$ _______________

439. $8\frac{2}{8} + 9\frac{3}{4} =$ _______________

440. $9\frac{1}{8} - 4\frac{3}{7} =$ _______________

441. $6\frac{2}{6} - 5\frac{3}{4} =$ _______________

442. $7\frac{1}{3} - 4\frac{1}{2} =$ _______________

443. $4\frac{8}{9} + 7\frac{3}{10} =$ _______________

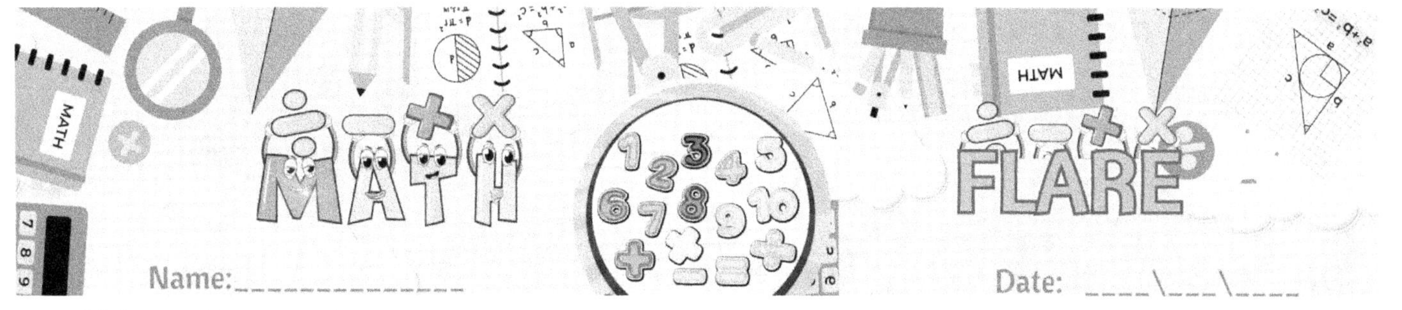

444. $9 \frac{3}{5} - 7 \frac{1}{3} =$ ___________________________

445. $2 \frac{5}{6} - 2 \frac{6}{9} =$ ___________________________

446. $5 \frac{1}{2} - 2 \frac{2}{4} =$ ___________________________

447. $7 \frac{2}{7} - 4 \frac{8}{10} =$ ___________________________

448. $8 \frac{3}{5} + 7 \frac{1}{8} =$ ___________________________

449. $9 \frac{4}{7} + 3 \frac{9}{10} =$ ___________________________

450. $6\frac{1}{4} + 2\frac{2}{3} =$ _______________

451. $8\frac{3}{8} - 5\frac{1}{5} =$ _______________

452. $5\frac{1}{7} - 4\frac{3}{6} =$ _______________

453. $5\frac{2}{9} + 9\frac{1}{2} =$ _______________

454. $9\frac{5}{6} - 4\frac{2}{8} =$ _______________

455. $9\frac{1}{3} - 8\frac{4}{7} =$ _______________

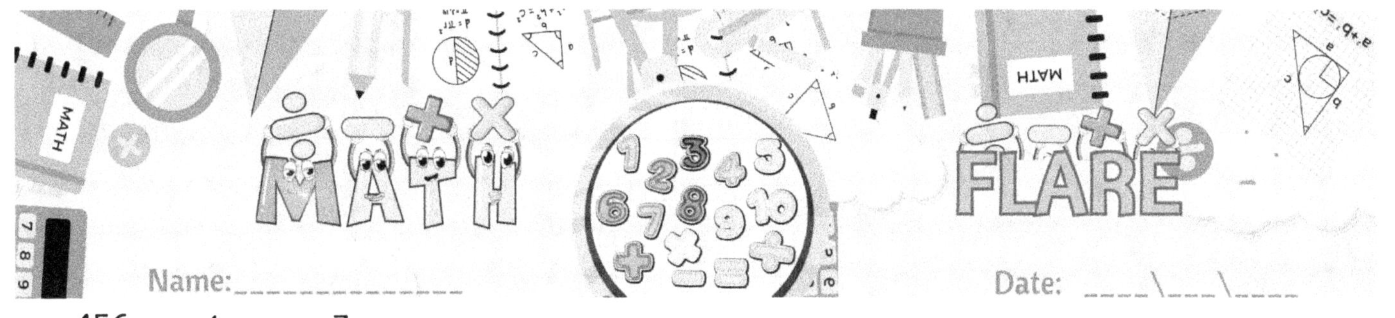

456. $9\frac{1}{2} + 2\frac{7}{10} =$ _______________________

457. $8\frac{4}{9} - 7\frac{1}{4} =$ _______________________

458. $9\frac{4}{5} - 4\frac{2}{8} =$ _______________________

459. $6\frac{1}{7} + 8\frac{1}{2} =$ _______________________

460. $1\frac{2}{6} + 2\frac{1}{5} =$ _______________________

461. $5\frac{8}{10} - 3\frac{2}{4} =$ _______________________

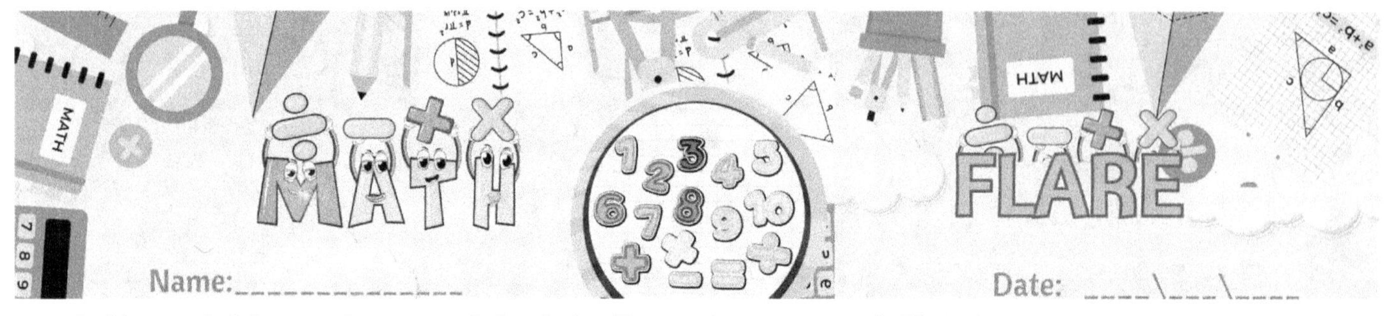

Mixed Numbers: Multiplication and Division

Calculate.

462. $4\frac{2}{5} \times 6\frac{4}{6} =$ _______________________

463. $7\frac{1}{2} \times 7\frac{3}{9} =$ _______________________

464. $6\frac{5}{7} \div 9\frac{1}{3} =$ _______________________

465. $5\frac{2}{8} \times 7\frac{8}{10} =$ _______________________

466. $6\frac{1}{4} \times 3\frac{1}{6} =$ _______________________

467. $2\frac{4}{5} \times 5\frac{1}{2} =$ _______________________

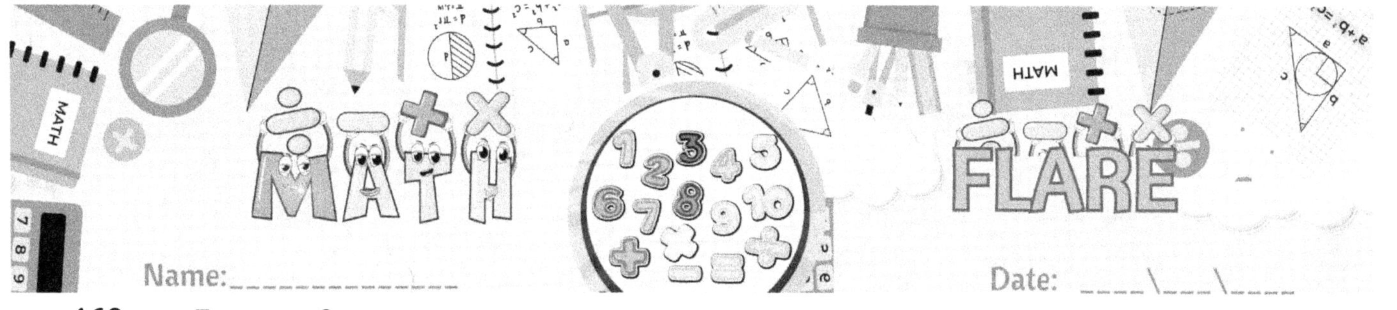

Name:_______________   Date: ____________

468. $7\frac{7}{9} \div 8\frac{2}{5} =$ _______________________________

469. $4\frac{2}{6} \div 8\frac{2}{4} =$ _______________________________

470. $4\frac{3}{10} \div 1\frac{3}{8} =$ _______________________________

471. $1\frac{2}{3} \times 7\frac{5}{7} =$ _______________________________

472. $1\frac{4}{7} \div 6\frac{4}{6} =$ _______________________________

473. $1\frac{7}{8} \times 1\frac{1}{2} =$ _______________________________

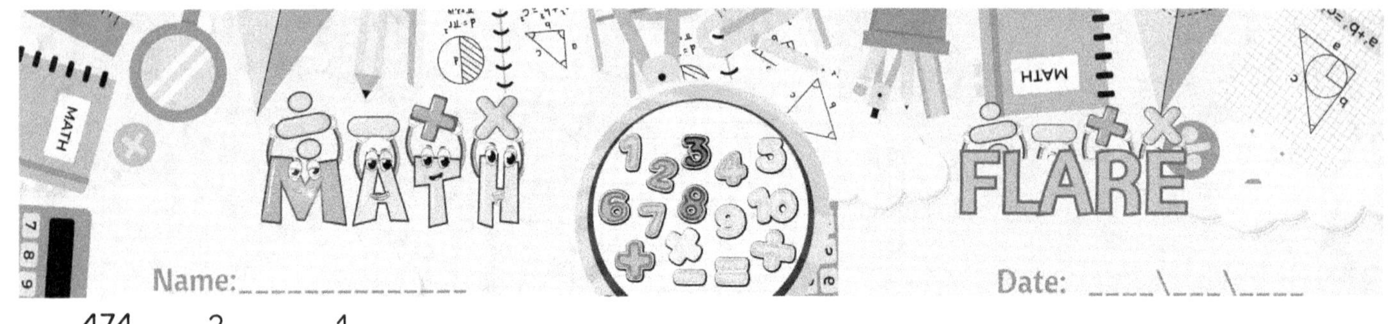

474. $9\frac{2}{3} \div 5\frac{1}{4} =$ _______________________________

475. $3\frac{2}{5} \times 7\frac{8}{9} =$ _______________________________

476. $7\frac{1}{10} \times 3\frac{7}{8} =$ _______________________________

477. $8\frac{3}{4} \div 5\frac{3}{5} =$ _______________________________

478. $6\frac{1}{2} \times 2\frac{4}{10} =$ _______________________________

479. $4\frac{4}{6} \div 9\frac{2}{3} =$ _______________________________

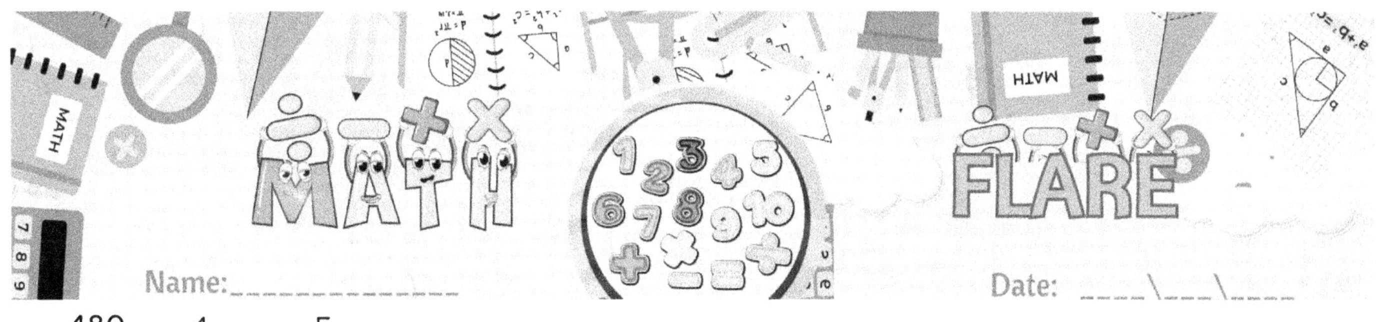

480. $7\frac{1}{7} \times 4\frac{5}{9} =$

481. $9\frac{1}{6} \times 2\frac{2}{3} =$

482. $9\frac{4}{10} \times 5\frac{4}{5} =$

483. $4\frac{3}{9} \times 4\frac{5}{8} =$

484. $7\frac{4}{7} \div 5\frac{1}{2} =$

485. $6\frac{3}{4} \div 6\frac{2}{4} =$

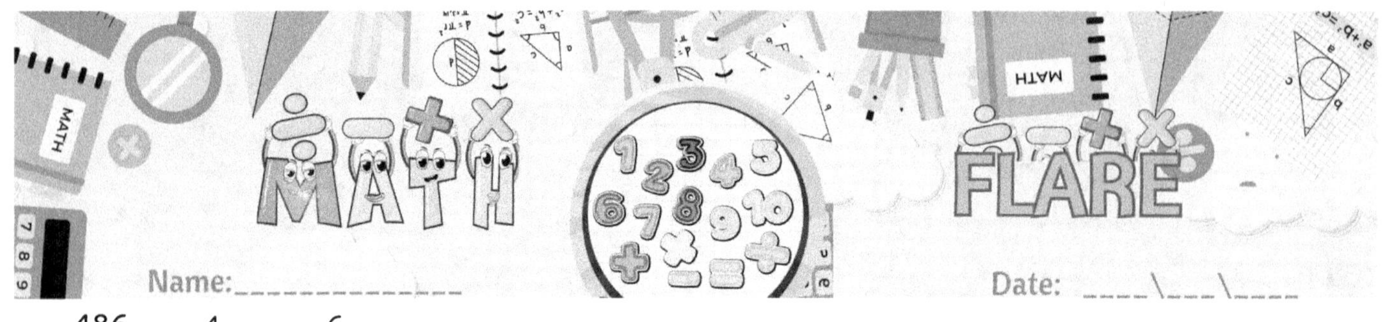

486. $6 \frac{1}{8} \times 9 \frac{6}{7} =$ ______________________

487. $4 \frac{2}{3} \times 5 \frac{1}{2} =$ ______________________

488. $7 \frac{3}{9} \div 5 \frac{8}{10} =$ ______________________

489. $7 \frac{5}{6} \div 8 \frac{3}{5} =$ ______________________

490. $3 \frac{1}{7} \div 4 \frac{4}{10} =$ ______________________

491. $2 \frac{3}{8} \times 2 \frac{2}{5} =$ ______________________

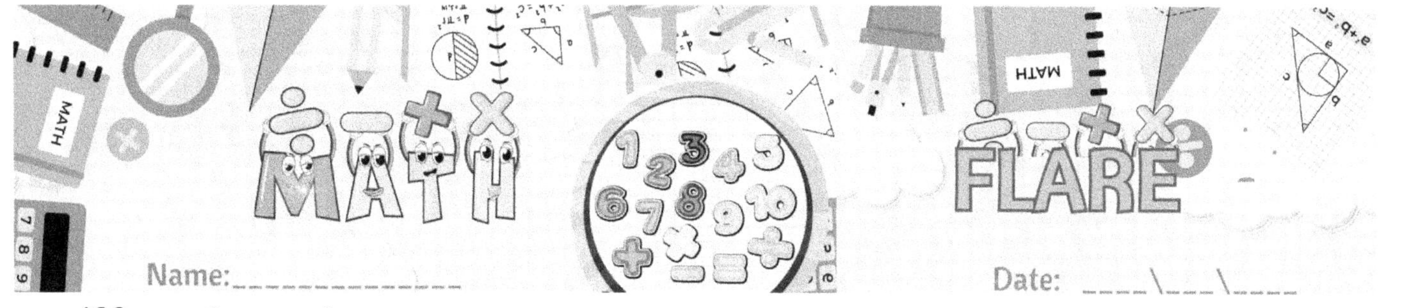

492. $8\frac{6}{9} \div 1\frac{2}{3} =$ _________________________

493. $4\frac{2}{4} \div 1\frac{1}{2} =$ _________________________

494. $6\frac{5}{6} \times 5\frac{2}{3} =$ _________________________

495. $2\frac{1}{2} \div 2\frac{4}{9} =$ _________________________

496. $5\frac{1}{10} \times 4\frac{4}{5} =$ _________________________

497. $1\frac{6}{8} \times 5\frac{3}{4} =$ _________________________

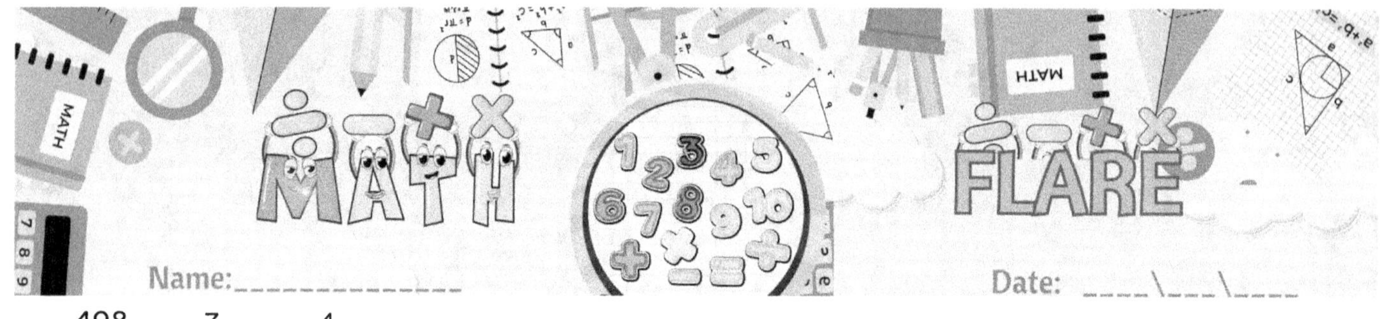

498. $5\frac{3}{6} \div 1\frac{1}{7} =$ _______________________

499. $6\frac{1}{3} \times 5\frac{2}{4} =$ _______________________

500. $6\frac{1}{8} \div 7\frac{3}{10} =$ _______________________

501. $8\frac{3}{5} \times 1\frac{6}{9} =$ _______________________

502. $2\frac{1}{2} \div 3\frac{2}{7} =$ _______________________

503. $9\frac{2}{6} \div 1\frac{2}{8} =$ _______________________

504. $2\frac{4}{5} \times 6\frac{2}{3} =$ _______________

505. $1\frac{2}{9} \div 5\frac{2}{4} =$ _______________

506. $2\frac{3}{6} \div 7\frac{3}{10} =$ _______________

507. $6\frac{1}{2} \div 3\frac{1}{7} =$ _______________

508. $1\frac{3}{9} \div 4\frac{5}{10} =$ _______________

509. $2\frac{3}{5} \times 1\frac{4}{7} =$ _______________

ANSWERS

Page 1:   Adding Decimals

1. 1,281.894	2. 1,094.808	3. 1,334.090	4. 1,581.771
5. 1,176.264	6. 1,266.102	7. 1,752.498	8. 1,335.679
9. 1,595.323	10. 877.480	11. 650.323	12. 814.763
13. 477.644	14. 1,542.190	15. 1,436.259	16. 1,058.562
17. 931.984	18. 1,333.570	19. 1,475.519	20. 1,279.132
21. 846.310	22. 1,671.090	23. 1,505.066	24. 1,059.561
25. 750.924	26. 947.216	27. 991.098	28. 1,250.125
29. 662.002	30. 797.567	31. 895.990	32. 426.051
33. 1,917.285	34. 979.361	35. 1,268.779	36. 315.271
37. 1,708.643	38. 1,209.141	39. 936.703	40. 1,235.300

Page 3:   Subtracting Decimals

41. 412.551	42. -231.541	43. -382.645	44. 58.280
45. 513.313	46. 212.283	47. -502.367	48. -149.512
49. 44.877	50. 527.234	51. 659.852	52. -234.892
53. -281.147	54. 125.195	55. -504.120	56. -189.115
57. 315.829	58. 214.690	59. 494.513	60. -8.524
61. 264.314	62. 174.748	63. 182.079	64. 158.603
65. 483.164	66. -501.582	67. 372.503	68. -106.421
69. 242.892	70. -368.284	71. 353.762	72. 67.745

73. 374.397   74. 111.694   75. -489.131   76. 366.245

77. 582.854   78. -114.366   79. -136.100   80. -271.703

Page 5:   Multiplying Decimals

81. 268.8468   82. 277.9476   83. 114.6100   84. 319.3515

85. 306.2280   86. 365.4000   87. 377.2000   88. 323.1312

89. 383.3864   90. 41.8300   91. 760.6395   92. 476.7210

93. 268.3450   94. 82.1201   95. 92.6528   96. 73.5210

97. 114.6894   98. 83.0812   99. 64.1250   100. 342.3627

101. 287.8484   102. 204.4354   103. 32.7120   104. 22.8140

105. 385.0058   106. 117.1398   107. 429.5025   108. 87.8982

109. 129.6256   110. 73.5852   111. 212.2044   112. 50.4432

113. 329.2950   114. 42.6246   115. 95.1735   116. 490.5292

117. 428.3520   118. 462.6872   119. 545.0172   120. 507.6752

121. 255.6137   122. 29.9128   123. 652.1565   124. 401.9840

125. 37.4816

Page 10:   Dividing Decimals

126. 2.06   127. 14.27   128. 9.9   129. 24.3   130. 5.17

131. 10.74   132. 33.05   133. 12.68   134. 9.44   135. 1.11

136. 5.2   137. 10.51   138. 7.64   139. 40.8   140. 3.33

141. 60.5   142. 7.09   143. 1.84   144. 7.0   145. 8.46

146. 17.8   147. 2.08   148. 41.45   149. 10.13   150. 3.4

151. 4.01   152. 16.1   153. 91.1   154. 27.0   155. 5.56

156. 4.71   157. 9.25   158. 2.19   159. 1.58   160. 11.56

161. 8.8

Page 14: Fractions Multiplication

162. 1/8   163. 1/60   164. 12/361   165. 6/11   166. 91/120

167. 3/8   168. 2/27   169. 9/70   170. 1/20   171. 40/51

172. 7/24   173. 4/7   174. 52/95   175. 4/13   176. 1/24

177. 5/9   178. 70/99   179. 8/25   180. 5/27   181. 32/55

182. 3/13   183. 1/6   184. 1/34   185. 1/9   186. 12/119

187. 5/24   188. 36/143   189. 7/120   190. 3/19   191. 17/60

192. 11/54   193. 3/8

Page 17: Fractions Division

194. 4/39   195. 4   196. 143/144   197. 1/2   198. 7/39

199. 5/13   200. 4/19   201. 17/165   202. 26/27   203. 2

204. 1/5   205. 1 1/14   206. 3 3/34   207. 1 2/3   208. 5/72

209. 8/9   210. 1 2/9   211. 156/187   212. 8   213. 2 2/15

214. 9/14   215. 1/9   216. 16/25   217. 1 17/21   218. 9/16

219. 17/168   220. 1 3/5   221. 1 1/7   222. 38/45   223. 7/72

224. 1 37/171   225. 1 1/8

Page 20: Fractions Multiplication Word Problems

226. 8/5   227. 2/15   228. 3/2   229. 7   230. 5   231. 8/3

232. 3/4   233. 8/5   234. 1/4   235. 5/3   236. 1/3   237. 3/5

238. 5   239. 8/3   240. 21/4   241. 2/3   242. 5/3   243. 2/3

244. 5/2   245. 27/5   246. 7/16

Page 27: Fractions Division Word Problems

247. 1/40   248. 5/21   249. 2/9   250. 1/4   251. 5/18   252. 1/30

253. 1/10   254. 1/4   255. 5/18   256. 1/8   257. 1/6   258. 1/9

259. 3/14   260. 1/4   261. 2/9   262. 1/4   263. 1/15   264. 4/15

265. 1 1/7   266. 3/20   267. 5/18

Page 34: Convert Fractions and Decimals

268. 0.38   269. 4/10   270. 0.85   271. 3/4   272. 1/6

273. 0.8   274. 0.39   275. 6/7   276. 0.8   277. 0.14

278. 0.22   279. 0.5   280. 12/17   281. 0.38   282. 0.33

283. 1/2   284. 0.36   285. 0.17   286. 0.93   287. 0.42

288. 6/20   289. 6/10   290. 4/12   291. 7/8   292. 1/16

293. 3/18   294. 0.27   295. 0.25   296. 11/14   297. 0.67

298. 2/11   299. 3/7   300. 0.06   301. 5/13   302. 0.68

303. 9/19   304. 10/14   305. 5/9   306. 0.78   307. 0.75

308. 0.71   309. 0.45   310. 9/17   311. 8/13   312. 2/10

313. 0.5   314. 15/20   315. 0.6

Page 38: Mixed Numbers

316. 77/12   317. 61/9   318. 49/10   319. 31/9   320. 7/2

321. 57/8   322. 15/2   323. 11/2   324. 19/4   325. 41/18

326. 13/10   327. 13/7   328. 35/4   329. 31/4   330. 16/9

331. 53/6   332. 22/7   333. 7/5   334. 13/2   335. 4/3

336. 19/12   337. 39/7   338. 39/8   339. 117/14   340. 7/2

341. 27/5   342. 77/18   343. 149/20   344. 3/2   345. 15/2

346. 62/9   347. 22/9   348. 61/8   349. 46/5   350. 26/3

351. 55/7   352. 17/7   353. 17/2   354. 13/2   355. 75/8

356. 4/3   357. 29/6   358. 41/6   359. 56/9   360. 28/5

361. 45/8   362. 86/9   363. 13/4   364. 9/2   365. 17/2

366. 38/5   367. 31/8   368. 17/4   369. 64/7   370. 16/3

371. 43/10

Page 42:   Mixed Numbers

372. 4 5/7   373. 1 5/7   374. 1 1/6   375. 5 7/10   376. 3 1/4

377. 3 11/20   378. 5 3/8   379. 1 7/12   380. 7 7/10   381. 9 4/7

382. 5 1/4   383. 6 3/4   384. 6 4/5   385. 4 2/5   386. 3 1/2

387. 1 1/7   388. 2 2/3   389. 2 2/3   390. 9 4/9   391. 2 1/4

392. 3 2/3   393. 3 3/5   394. 4 3/20   395. 2 3/10   396. 4 7/9

397. 4 5/6   398. 8 1/2   399. 2 1/4   400. 7 3/20   401. 4 7/9

402. 1 3/14   403. 4 3/4   404. 1 3/8   405. 7 1/3   406. 6 2/3

407. 5 2/5   408. 7 15/16   409. 5 6/7   410. 4 1/3   411. 2 1/9

412. 9 1/3   413. 7 2/5

Page 45:   Mixed Numbers: Addition and Subtraction

414. 1 1/6	415. 5 3/14	416. 11 8/15	417. 1 1/4
418. 8 11/12	419. 3	420. 5 5/14	421. 11 7/9
422. 7 29/30	423. 8 7/12	424. 15 17/56	425. 1 13/15
426. 3 5/6	427. 15 3/14	428. 6 2/3	429. 15 17/20
430. 14/15	431. 11 17/18	432. 2 7/12	433. 9 39/70
434. 2 1/8	435. 15 9/10	436. 16 1/6	437. 1 1/21
438. 7 7/10	439. 18	440. 4 39/56	441. 7/12
442. 2 5/6	443. 12 17/90	444. 2 4/15	445. 1/6
446. 3	447. 2 17/35	448. 15 29/40	449. 13 33/70
450. 8 11/12	451. 3 7/40	452. 9/14	453. 14 13/18
454. 5 7/12	455. 16/21	456. 12 1/5	457. 1 7/36
458. 5 11/20	459. 14 9/14	460. 3 8/15	461. 2 3/10

Page 53:   Mixed Numbers: Multiplication and Division

462. 29 1/3	463. 55	464. 141/196	465. 40 19/20
466. 19 19/24	467. 15 2/5	468. 25/27	469. 26/51
470. 3 7/55	471. 12 6/7	472. 33/140	473. 2 13/16
474. 1 53/63	475. 26 37/45	476. 27 41/80	477. 1 9/16
478. 15 3/5	479. 14/29	480. 32 34/63	481. 24 4/9
482. 54 13/25	483. 20 1/24	484. 1 29/77	485. 1 1/26
486. 60 3/8	487. 25 2/3	488. 1 23/87	489. 235/258

490. 5/7   491. 5 7/10   492. 5 1/5   493. 3

494. 38 13/18   495. 1 1/44   496. 24 12/25   497. 10 1/16

498. 4 13/16   499. 34 5/6   500. 245/292   501. 14 1/3

502. 35/46   503. 7 7/15   504. 18 2/3   505. 2/9

506. 25/73   507. 2 3/44   508. 8/27   509. 4 3/35